AN INTRODUCTION TO POLO

The Correct Position in the Saddle

AN INTRODUCTION TO
POLO

BY 'MARCO'

PREFACE BY

ADMIRAL OF THE FLEET
THE EARL MOUNTBATTEN OF BURMA
K.G., P.C., G.C.B., O.M., G.C.S.I., G.C.I.E., G.C.V.O., D.S.O., F.R.S.

J. A. ALLEN : LONDON

ISBN 0 85131 142 3

First published, May, 1931
by Country Life Limited
Second Impression, 1931
Second Edition, 1937
Third Edition, 1950
Fourth Edition, 1960
Fifth Edition, 1965

© Sixth Edition, Royal Naval Saddle Club 1976

Published in 1976 by
J. A. Allen & Company Limited,
1, Lower Grosvenor Place,
London, SW1W 0EL

Printed in Great Britain by
Redwood Burn Limited
Trowbridge & Esher

CONTENTS

List of Plates — ix
List of Figures — xi
Introduction to the Sixth Edition (1976) — xiii

PART ONE

I. Horsemanship — 3

  Seat—Exercises—The Aids—'Hands'—Stopping—Reining Back—Changing Legs—Aids for Changing Legs—Turning—Riding-Off—Placing the Pony—Cure for Lameness

II. Equipment — 15

  Sticks: Length of the Stick—Types of Handle—The Slings—Shape, Dimensions, and Weight of the Head—Materials for the Shaft of the Stick—Materials for the Head of the Stick—Selection of Materials for Shafts and Heads—The Stick recommended to the Beginner—The Care of Sticks
  Saddlery: Saddle—Bridle—Standing Martingale—Boots—Tail-Bandage—Stable Gear
  Dress
  Polo Pit, and Wooden Horse

III. Striking — 31

  The Four Fundamental Strokes—The Rest Position—The Brace—The Grip of the Stick—The Ideal Stroke—The Swing—Learning the Swing, 'by numbers'—The Off-Side Forehand Swing—Learning to Hit Off-Side Forehanders—Hitting when Mounted—The Off-Side Backhand Swing—Learning to Hit Off-Side Backhanders—Starting to Play—The Near-Side Forehand Stroke—The Near-Side Backhand Stroke—Loft and Length—The Effect of a Rolling Ball—Cut and Pulled Strokes—The Diamond Rule—The Off-Side Under-the-Neck Stroke—The Near-Side Under-the-Neck Stroke—'Fancy' Strokes—Quickness in Striking

CONTENTS

PART TWO

IV. THE GAME — 61
The Team—The Umpires and Referee—The Duration of Play—Scoring—Handicapping—Indoor Polo—The Throw-In—The Game opens Out—Ball Out of Play—Crossing—Dangerous Riding—Rough Handling—Misuse of Stick—Appealing for Fouls—Dismounted Player—Penalties—The First Game

V. TEAM PLAY — 72
Forming a Team—Discipline on the Ground—Discipline off the Ground—The Basic Principles of Team Play—Passing the Ball—Waiting, and Calling, for a Pass—Centering—Shooting at Goal—Riding-Off and Stick-Hooking—Combined Practice—Advice to Players, Individually—General Advice—Duties of the Captain—Drawing-up an Organisation

VI. SPECIMEN ORGANISATION — 89
ATTACK: Positions at the Throw-in—Normal Attack-Formations—Positions at the 30-Yard, 40-Yard, 60-Yard, and Free Hits—Positions at the Hit-in—Special Examples
DEFENCE: Positions at the Throw-in—Positions at the Hit-in—Positions at the 30-Yard, 40-Yard, 60-Yard, and Free Hits
INFORMATIVE CALLING: List of Calls
CONSIDERATIONS OF PONY-POWER

APPENDICES

APPENDIX I	STABLE MANAGEMENT	113
APPENDIX II	HISTORY OF THE RULES	119
APPENDIX III	THE HURLINGHAM POLO ASSOCIATION RULES OF POLO	121
APPENDIX IV	THE HURLINGHAM POLO ASSOCIATION NOTES ON THE RULES	140
APPENDIX V	H.P.A. DIRECTIVE ON RULES RE SUBSTITUTION	150
APPENDIX VI	THE UNITED STATES POLO ASSOCIATION RULES OF POLO	152
APPENDIX VII	THE UNITED STATES POLO ASSOCIATION GUIDE FOR UMPIRES	170
APPENDIX VIII	HURLINGHAM POLO ASSOCIATION AND UNITED STATES POLO ASSOCIATION PENALTIES COMPARED	177

CONTENTS

Appendix IX	Rules and Tactics *by Thomas Hitchcock, Jr.*	180
Bibliography		183
Index		185

PLATES

The Correct Position in the Saddle		*Frontispiece*
I. The Correct Position for Stopping		*Facing page* 8
II. Types of Stick		,, ,, 18
III. The Grip		,, ,, 19
IV. The Off-Side Forehander (Superimposed)	⎫	
V. The Off-Side Backhander (Superimposed)	⎬ *Facing page* 34	
VI. The Near-Side Forehander (Superimposed)	⎫	
VII. The Near-Side Backhander (Superimposed)	⎬ *Facing page* 35	
VIII. The Off-Side Forehander (Wodehouse)		
IX. The Off-Side Forehander (Wodehouse)		
X. The Off-Side Forehander (Guest)		
XI. The Off-Side Backhander (Wodehouse)		
XII. The Off-Side Backhander (Guest)		
XIII. The Off-Side Under-the-Neck Stroke (Wodehouse)		
XIV. The Near-Side Forehander (Guest)	⎬ *After page* 57	
XV. The Near-Side Forehander (Wodehouse)		
XVI. The Near-Side Forehander (Guest)		
XVII. The Near-Side Backhander (Wodehouse)		
XVIII. The Near-Side Backhander (Guest)		
XIX. The Near-Side Under-the-Neck-Stroke (Wodehouse)		
XX. The Near-Side Under-the-Neck Stroke (Guest)		
XXI. Supplementary Views (Both Players)		

FIGURES

1.	The Points of a Pony	5
2.	The Aids for Turning to the Left	12
3.	Cross-sections of Stick-heads	20
4.	Details for a Polo-Pit	28
5.	The Wooden Horse	29
6.	The Twelve Principal Strokes	32
7.	Topping the Ball through Pressing	36
8.	The Off-Side Forehand Swing	38
9.	The Off-Side Backhand Swing	43
10.	The Near-Side Forehand Swing	47
11.	The Near-Side Backhand Swing	49
12.	Position of Ball for Loft and for Length	50
13.	The Diamond Rule	54
14.	The Game Opens Out	65
15.	The Advantage of Centering	78
16.	The Reason for Centering Early	79
17.	Number 1 meeting the Ball at the Throw-In	90
18.	Number 2 meeting the Ball at the Throw-In	91
19.	Number 3 meeting the Ball at the Throw-In	92
20.	The Back meeting the Ball at the Throw-In	93
21.	Normal Attack-Formations	94
22.	The 40-Yard Hit	95
23.	The 60-Yard Hit	96
24.	The Free Hit	97
25.	Own Hit-In	98
26.	Attack from the Boards	99
27.	Two Players on the Ball	100
28.	Man Nearest Enemy Goal in Possession	101
29.	Opponents meeting the Ball at the Throw-In	103
30.	Opponents' Hit-In	104

INTRODUCTION TO THE SIXTH EDITION (1976)

It is now forty-five years ago since this book was originally written and published in 1931. In the Preface that the late Earl of Kimberley (who gained his fame as an international polo-player while still Lord Wodehouse) contributed to the First Edition, he wrote:

> On reading the book I was interested to find that it contained perhaps the most reasoned and progressive introduction to the game from first principles that I had ever read. No attempt was made to investigate the theory of horsemanship, but the beginner could learn enough of the aids and their application, to control a pony on the polo ground. The chapter on striking the ball, on the other hand, contained detailed analysis of strokes, which turned out to be the most serious attempt to attack this problem which I had yet come across. The analysis sets out many simple truths, I found, such as considerations for lofting the ball, which are generally overlooked, and from which few players would fail to benefit.

In my travels since World War II I have been to many polo clubs in all five continents and have been continually surprised to find early editions of this book still in use in those clubs. I have received numerous requests for further copies which could not be supplied as the book was out of print. So I am very glad that J. A. Allen is now printing a Sixth Edition with the Rules of Polo brought right up to date.

In 1931 I gave the copyright to the Royal Naval Polo Association (now amalgamated with the Royal Naval Saddle Club) and as its President join the members in expressing the hope that the Sixth Edition will prove a help to all those who are taking up this most fascinating and thrilling of games.

Mountbatten of Burma
A.F.

PART ONE

CHAPTER ONE
HORSEMANSHIP

BEFORE you start to play polo, make sure that you are able to concentrate on your hitting without having to be busy riding. If you have never ridden in your life, begin by taking lessons from someone competent to give them, for you can't satisfactorily teach yourself. If you have ridden before, but don't feel sufficiently secure in the saddle to start playing, ride whenever you get the chance.

In either case you would do well to study the following remarks on horsemanship, and try to understand the theories that underlie your practice.

Don't forget that your pony, when you play him in a game of polo, is being made to do things he would never attempt to do if he were left to his own devices, and that you are making him do these things, unnatural to him in the first place, with the added weight of a man on his back. If you notice, in reading the following instructions, that the pony is sometimes compelled to do things in ways that are evidently not the ones he would choose, remember that he is not the best judge, any more than you yourself would be, of how to accomplish feats to which the normal man had no inclination.

Your pony will have received long and careful schooling, to accustom him to the idea of what he will be asked to do, and to the way in which he will be expected to do it, and he will have to be kept up to the mark and prevented from falling back into the natural habits of which he has been broken.

As a beginner, however, you will not be expected to school your pony, or to correct his faults (if any should develop) yourself. It has been assumed in this chapter that you have been riding a made pony (*i.e.* one who is already schooled and trained for polo); and for this reason you will find no programme of schooling, and no instructions for correcting and improving him. The following advice is concerned entirely with the knowledge of riding that you will need for playing polo, even though the procedure may in some respects diverge from that which you would have had to follow if you had been dealing with an unmade, or 'green' pony.

HORSEMANSHIP

Figure 1 shows the points of the pony; the under-surface of his foot; and the off-side view of the inside of his mouth, as a six-year-old.

SEAT

A good seat is the fundamental necessity in riding, and especially in polo, since many of the shots have to be taken leaning right out of the saddle, and at a gallop.

The frontispiece will show you the correct position in the saddle. Study this carefully; note the forward position of the body, and how the legs are kept close in, and the heels well back. The length of your stirrup-leathers should just allow you to place your clenched fist between the saddle and the fork of your legs, when you rise in the stirrups.

The best way to achieve a firm seat in the saddle is to ride regularly without stirrups. This will improve your balance, and it will also develop a set of muscles that are hardly ever used except on horseback. Every time you ride, cross your stirrups over the withers (see Figure 1) and ride for a short time without them. But don't overdo this at first, for in the early stages the riding muscle is easily strained; it takes weeks to develop, and you will risk seriously injuring it if you try to force the pace. Always replace the stirrups, therefore, at the first sign of tiredness.

Extend the time of riding without them gradually, until you can do this for a quarter-of-an-hour daily without over-tiring yourself.

Start doing this at a walk and leave trotting till later.

EXERCISES

In polo, it is all-important that you should be able to move the upper and lower parts of your body entirely independently. In order to make a shot, or to 'ride off' another player, you must be able to move the body freely from the waist, in any direction, while continuing to ride the pony correctly with your legs, as if your body had not moved. In order to do this, it is obvious that you will need to be exceptionally supple at the waist. The following suppling exercises are recommended:

(1) Stand with the feet six inches apart. Keeping the knees straight, bend forward and rest your knuckles on the ground behind the heels.

(2) Stand with the feet apart and the arms stretched out sideways. Keeping the knees straight, bend the trunk to the left as far as you can

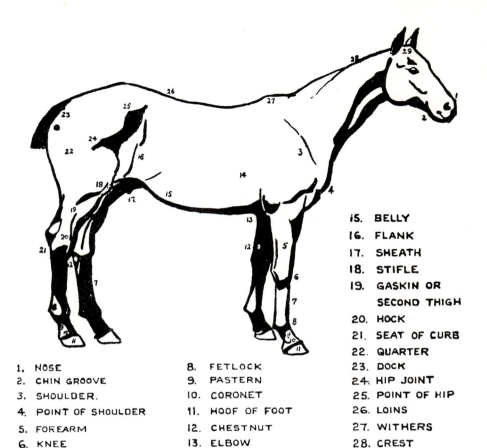

1. NOSE
2. CHIN GROOVE
3. SHOULDER.
4. POINT OF SHOULDER
5. FOREARM
6. KNEE
7. CANNON BONE
8. FETLOCK
9. PASTERN
10. CORONET
11. HOOF OF FOOT
12. CHESTNUT
13. ELBOW
14. RIBS
15. BELLY
16. FLANK
17. SHEATH
18. STIFLE
19. GASKIN OR SECOND THIGH
20. HOCK
21. SEAT OF CURB
22. QUARTER
23. DOCK
24. HIP JOINT
25. POINT OF HIP
26. LOINS
27. WITHERS
28. CREST
29. POLL

UNDER SURFACE OF FOOT

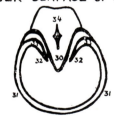

30. FROG
31. WALL OF FOOT
32. SEAT OF CORN
33. BARS
34. CLEFT OF FROG

INSIDE OF MOUTH

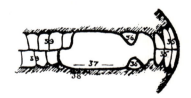

35. INCISORS, UPPER AND LOWER
36. TUSHES, UPPER AND LOWER
37. BARS OF THE MOUTH
38. SEAT OF USUAL BIT INJURY
39. MOLARS, UPPER AND LOWER

FIG. I. THE POINTS OF A PONY

without leaning forward. Then, keeping your right heel on the ground, twist the body round until the right hand touches the ground behind the left leg. Resume your original position, and repeat the exercise to your right.

Do both these exercises a dozen times daily, until you can do them without effort; after that you need only do them before a match.

As soon as you feel sufficiently secure in the saddle, start doing suppling exercises mounted, taking care to keep the reins in the bridle-hand (*i.e.* the left hand) all the time, and in the correct position:

(3) Ride with your right hand holding the right stirrup.
(4) Ride with your right hand holding the left stirrup.
(5) Turn in the saddle to your right, while riding along, and rest your right hand on the near (*i.e.* the left-hand) side of the pony's hindquarters.
(6) Turn to the left and try to touch the same spot as before, again with your right hand.

Do these exercises first at a walk, later working up to a canter. It is not easy to keep control of the pony when you are riding in these positions, so you are recommended to start the exercises in a riding-school, or manège.

To strengthen your wrists and forearms, you can carry a 'squash-ball' about in your pocket, and at odd moments squeeze and relax it a few times. Another good plan is to have a broken polo-stick cut down, and a leaden weight fixed on it as a head, but about eighteen inches below the handle; and to swing this at odd moments.

THE AIDS

The code of signals by which you convey your wishes to your pony is known as the 'aids'; and these signals are conveyed by means of your *voice*, *hands* and *legs*, and by the *disposal of the weight of your body*.

The secret of success in applying the aids is to do so evenly and smoothly.

The *voice* is used mainly for warning the pony that he is about to be made to stop.

The *legs*, from the knee down, are used to control the quarters and hindlegs of the pony; and the theory of the application of the leg-aid is that the pony will move away from any pressure that you apply with the leg to his side just behind the girth. For instance, if you apply the right leg, the pony will move his quarters to the left; unless his quarters are already swinging round to the right, in which case the application of the right leg will check this swing and anchor the pony's quarters. If you apply both legs simultaneously, the pony will move forward to try and escape from their pressure; unless you put tension on the reins, and the pressure of the bit on his mouth prevents him from moving forward, in which case he will move backwards. Spurs make the leg-aid more effective.

The *disposal of the weight of your body* is used in stopping or turning the pony, and helps to enforce your wish by placing your weight where it will be most useful to him.

The *hands* are used to control the forehand of the pony (*i.e.* that part of him that is front of the saddle), by means of the reins, which either press against the pony's neck or on the bit in his mouth.

'HANDS'

The term 'hands', of course, embraces far more than the aid, having reference also to the instinctive sympathy that the good rider is able to establish at once between his horse and himself. This quality is sometimes inborn, but is more often acquired, and should be attainable by any really keen horseman.

While you are riding without stirrups and doing suppling exercises, it does not matter so much what sort of mouth your mount has; but as soon as you feel fairly supple and secure you should make every effort to get hold of a pony with a good mouth, and start to develop your hands.

People are chary of lending a good pony to a beginner, for a rider with bad hands will spoil a pony with a good mouth. But if you continue to ride hirelings with bad mouths you cannot expect to acquire good hands; it is essential, therefore, that you should endeavour to procure a decent mount.

A good mouth must necessarily be a sensitive one, susceptible to the lightest signal transmitted to it through the bit and reins. Unnecessary force in passing these signals will cause the pony pain, against which he will usually fight; and if you reply to this with still more force, a vicious circle will be set up and the wretched animal's mouth will be hardened and spoilt.

It will help you acquire lightness of hand if you ride with bent fingers, wrist, and forearm, for all these will be acting as shock absorbers to the pony's mouth. You can do this best by riding with as long a rein as possible (consistent with control); playing with your pony's mouth the whole time; and using your wrist and fingers as much as possible. Practise this, at first, with two reins in each hand, but later with all four in the bridle-hand.

HORSEMANSHIP

STOPPING

The beginner is usually exasperated on being told that the pony will not pull at him unless he pulls at the pony, yet there is a great deal of truth in this statement.

If, for instance, you will imagine yourself trying to stop a bicycle by tugging at the handle-bars, you will see at once how futile this would be. The handle-bars would merely pull back at you with an 'equal and opposite' force, and you might succeed in bending them, but you certainly would not manage to stop the bicycle.

In the same way, you will find you can't stop a pony by using brute force and pulling on the reins (which, in any case, are there to convey your wishes to your pony, and not to enforce them by violence). The brake, which would have stopped your hypothetical bicycle so easily, is applied in the pony's case by using certain aids which all ponies have been taught to recognise as a signal to stop.

In order to stop a pony properly, you must first of all squeeze hard with both legs close to the girth, and feel the reins. This brings his hocks under him and lifts his head, and is called 'collecting' him. Take care, while squeezing him, to sit well back and down in the saddle, and to lean back rather than forward. In order to come to a stop, a pony has to throw his weight backwards, just as a running man would have to; and by leaning slightly back, you will be helping him to shift his weight as far as possible from the forelegs to the hindlegs.

When you have collected your pony, your next action (which is so often the first, or indeed the *only*, action the indifferent rider will take) should be to tighten and slacken the reins once or twice lightly, by bending the fingers and wrist as already explained.

The correct position for stopping the pony is shown in Plate I.

Practise stopping the pony first from a walk, later from a trot, and finally from a canter or gallop.

Some ponies dislike pulling up sharp from an enjoyable gallop more than they dislike the discomfort caused by a mild signal to stop. In such cases slightly stronger pressure, or a slightly severer bit, may be used, so as to increase the discomfort until it outweighs the annoyance of having to stop. But you should resort to this only if careful schooling has failed to make your pony more amenable to a mild bit.

A pony that has been stopping well may suddenly take to running-on, or stopping badly. If his mouth is persistently jerked hard he may be ruined

PLATE I *The Correct Position for Stopping*

HORSEMANSHIP

for life. Examine your pony's mouth, if he behaves like this, and if that is the seat of trouble it must be seen to at once. You should also look at his legs, for such behaviour is often a sign of impending lameness, and means that the jar of stopping is proving more painful than the bit. In either case rest and treatment are essential.

Some ponies, notably 'barbs' (*i.e.* those from the Barbary Coast), develop a bad habit of anticipating the rider's wishes by stopping and turning as soon as they feel that he is shaping for a backhander. This will, obviously, spoil the stroke. But the habit can be broken by placing half a dozen balls in a straight line, thirty or forty yards apart, and riding down in a straight line, at a gallop, hitting backhanders, without allowing the pony to ease-up or turn.

Conversely, if your pony becomes too excited when you are knocking a ball about, and starts pulling each time you hit the ball, through a wish to chase it, stop him, and rein back before you reach the ball for the next shot. The process of reining back which is explained below, should be repeated as often as necessary.

REINING BACK

Your pony requires suppling exercises just as much as you do; and the exercise which does the average pony the most good is the rein-back (*i.e.* making him walk backwards in a straight line). This exercise also teaches the pony to bring his hind legs under him, which is the correct position for him when stopping. (Make a point of noticing also, whether reining back does not improve your pony's mouth.)

To rein back when your pony is at a halt, feel your reins (*i.e.* put a mild pressure on them), at the same time keeping his hocks under him by pressing your legs gently against his sides. So long as the hand-aid is stronger than the leg one, the pony will rein back in a collected manner. Don't let him take more than a few steps to the rear at a time, nor allow him to run back out of control.

To halt the pony while reining back, cease the pressure on the reins and ease the pressure of the legs.

If the pony leans on the bit and won't come back at once, keep a slight pressure on the reins and squeeze him intermittently with your legs until he does so. In a stubborn case you may have to wait as long as a minute before the pony gives in; but you must on no account lose your patience and job him in the mouth.

HORSEMANSHIP

CHANGING LEGS

If you watch a pony canter, you will notice that he consistently brings one foreleg to the ground just in front of the other, and a fraction of a second later. (This can be verified by Plates XVId and XVIc respectively which follow page 57.)

Similarly, you will see that he normally brings down the hind leg on the *same* side just in front of the other hindleg (Plate XVIc), and just afterwards (Plate XVIb). A pony is said to be cantering with near foreleg, or the off foreleg 'leading', depending on which leg he brings down in front. The pony shown in Plate XVI is leading with the off fore.

At first, when mounted, you may be uncertain with which leg your pony is leading. You can easily find out, however, by leaning out over the pony's shoulder and observing which leg is coming down in front. (In the same way you can see which hindleg is leading by looking under your pony's belly.) But you must learn as soon as possible to tell by the rhythm of the canter, without having to look down; for if you develop the bad habit of craning forward to watch your pony change legs in front, you will be throwing your weight forward at the wrong moment. This will encourage your pony to turn on the forehand (*i.e.* by pivoting on his forelegs), which, as explained in the section of this chapter which deals with Turning, is the incorrect way for him to turn. Throwing your weight forward will also cause your pony to change his legs in front without changing them behind. If he does this he will sprawl about and be unbalanced (which is called 'cantering disunited'); and he will probably be 'caught on the wrong leg' if suddenly required to do anything.

Start the change with the hindlegs. Whereas a slack pony will very often not change behind if he is allowed to change in front first, you will find that making a pony change behind first will force him to change in front as well.

The exact moment at which the pony can make the change is just after his leading foreleg has come to the ground, and his hindlegs are both in the air (see Plate XVIe). The aids should be applied *just* before this, and the pony will bring down first whichever hindleg they indicate. There can be no cast-iron rule about the correct moment for their application, for the lapse of time necessary varies with the responsiveness of the pony, and this depends upon his sensory nerves. You can, therefore, only learn by practice to *feel* exactly when to apply the aids.

HORSEMANSHIP

AIDS FOR CHANGING LEGS

In order to make your pony, cantering with his Near fore leading, change to the Off fore leading.

(*a*) Collect him, by squeezing with both legs and lightly feeling the reins.

(*b*) Apply your left leg strongly, just behind the girth. He will then put down his near hindleg first.

(*c*) Lean back, and slightly to the right. This will make him bring his off hindleg forward to support your weight.

(*d*) Carry your left hand over to the right, feeling the left rein gently, so that he turns his head slightly to the left. This will cramp the left side of his neck and forehand, but will encourage him to reach out with his off-fore leading.

In order to change from Off fore leading to Near fore leading, reverse these aids.

When you feel that the pony is changing his legs, you must instantly cease applying the aids, or else he will turn in the direction of what is now the leading leg.

In practice, few players bother to make their ponies lead with a particular leg, and only use the aids for changing legs when they wish to turn. When turning, the pony should always be leading with the *inner* leg. If he is allowed to lead with the outer foreleg, this will be crossing in front of his inner foreleg at each stride, and sooner or later he will trip up and fall.

TURNING

Learn to turn your pony *on the hocks* (*i.e.* on his hindlegs).

You can also turn him on the forehand (*i.e.* on his forelegs), or about the centre; but these ways are not safe, as the pony is apt to cross his legs and bring you down, even when he is leading with the correct leg.

Before attempting to turn your pony, especially when galloping, 'collect' him as you would for stopping him: squeeze hard with both legs, and tighten the reins once or twice, while sitting well down and back in the saddle.

Figure 2 shows the correct position for the turn on the hocks.

You will find that the aids for turning your pony to the left are very similar to those for making him change from off-fore to near-fore leading.

HORSEMANSHIP

In turning to the left apply the right leg strongly, pressing it further back while easing the pressure of the left leg; at the same time, draw your bridle-hand *backward and to the left*; and lean inwards.

The application of the leg will anchor the pony's quarters; if you omit this, he may pivot round on his forehand. The act of drawing your bridle-hand backward and to the left will tend to cause the tension of the reins on each side of the pony's mouth to be in the direction of his near hindleg; and this will bring him back on to his hocks. By leaning inwards you will be disposing of the weight of your body in a way that will best enforce your wish and be most useful to your pony: (for even a bicycle, if you took your hands

FIG. 2. THE AIDS FOR TURNING TO THE LEFT

off the handle-bars, would have to follow round in the direction in which you had leaned over!).

In turning to the Right, reverse the aids, applying the left leg, drawing your bridle-hand backward and to the Right, and again leaning inwards.

In turning and checking simultaneously, you will of course lean *inwards and backward*.

Straighten out, in every case, by easing the reins and equalising the pressure of the legs.

Sometimes a green pony will not respond sufficiently to the backward tension on the reins, and will need to be *led round* by the left (or 'direct') rein, when turning left-handed, with the right (or 'indirect') rein slackened. This slackening of the backward tension will have the effect of removing the

HORSEMANSHIP

backward pull on to the hocks, and will allow the pony to turn on the forehand. If your pony shows this tendency, you must have him schooled out of it.

Some ponies canter more readily with one leg leading than the other, and consequently turn more easily in the direction of that leg. This tendency can be rectified by making your pony turn more often in the other direction, and by taking care to make him change his legs properly.

When you come to play in fast tournament polo, you will find that the best way to turn your pony, if you want him to bring you back again into the game at high speed, is to *swing* him.

In order to do this, check him imperceptibly, to enable him to change legs, if this is necessary; then turn him sharply in the desired direction, galloping him round in the smallest possible space, and urging him as you turn to increase, rather than decrease, speed. Keep the outer leg applied hard, to counteract any tendency, at this speed, to turn on the forehand.

RIDING-OFF

In polo, you will often find that you need to 'ride-off' another player, either to prevent him from reaching the ball, or to prevent him from pushing you over it.

A considerable degree of horsemanship is required before your possibly unwillingly pony can be made to push against another; but you can make him do this by carrying over the reins, applying the outer leg hard, sitting squarely down in the saddle, and riding your pony into the other one.

Remember that it is the *shock of your pony's weight* being thrown against him that will force the other pony off the line.

It is important that you should try to get sufficient 'lead' on your adversary, before closing with him, to ensure that your knee will be in front of his at the moment of impact, for this will give your pony an obvious advantage.

When you have made contact, lean well out from the saddle, and drive the point of your shoulder into your opponent's side. Keep your shoulder well below his if he retaliates, and see that your elbow is in to your side (see Field Rule 18 on pages 129 and 160).

You will need a good deal of practice if you wish to become good at riding-off, and you should, therefore, try to practise this with a mounted friend.

HORSEMANSHIP

PLACING THE PONY

Select marks (such as tufts of grass, stones, etc.), and decide to ride close by them on the near side or on the off. At first you may do this holding the reins in both hands, but you should soon practise with the reins held in the bridle-hand only, and use your legs to help guide the pony. In this way you will learn to place him for shots, which you will find very useful when you start hitting.

You were told at the beginning of this chapter not to start playing until you are able to *concentrate on the ball and the game.* You will not have time in a fast game to remember what the book says about riding, and act on it; but if you have paid due attention to the foregoing remarks, you will have developed good habits, and you will have accustomed your pony to those habits, and taught him to act as one with you.

After the Appendices you will find a Bibliography of polo and riding, which you are recommended to read. The more carefully and conscientiously you have studied the rules of horesmanship, the more successfully you will be able to apply them when you have to do so automatically.

CURE FOR LAMENESS

The strain of stopping and turning very quickly, or a collision, not infrequently causes lameness in polo ponies.

Before World War II a Naval physiotherapist, used to cure members of the Royal Navy Polo Team of sprains, strains and contusions by applying rythmic muscular contractions, induced by Faradism to the injury. In 1939 the Captain of the team persuaded him (now Sir Charles Strong) to try the same treatment on lame polo ponies. Its success was phenomenal but the War delayed its development. Its value in curing lameness has now been proved over and over again.

Any Veterinary Surgeon in possession of Strong's Equine Veterinary Apparatus (known as S.E.V.A.) can use this on the affected parts. If this is done skilfully on the day of injury, or as soon after as possible, there is an overwhelming chance of a very quick cure enabling the pony to be brought back into play much sooner than by any other known method. (See page 117).

CHAPTER TWO

EQUIPMENT

STICKS

THE choice of your stick (or mallet, as it is called in America), is an important factor in determining how well you will eventually be able to strike; and you should therefore experiment as much as you can with different sorts of sticks, until you are reasonably certain which suits you the best. In choosing a stick, the following considerations are involved:

> Length of the stick;
> Type of handle;
> Shape, dimensions, and weight of the head;
> Materials for the shaft of the stick;
> Materials for the head of the stick.

To go into these considerations as thoroughly as you should will entail a greater knowledge of your strokes, and of your capacity for hitting, than you are likely to have as a beginner. But when your striking starts to improve, you will begin to see what qualities you require in your sticks; and you can then discard, if you wish, the type of stick recommended to you and use the information which follows, to improve upon your choice of stick and improve your striking.

For the time being you will only be able to decide two things yourself: the length of stick you need, and the 'feel' of stick that you find pleasant. But if you read the following pages, you will realise when you come to page 23, and find what stick you are recommended, why that particular type of stick has been chosen.

It will be hard to determine what you think of the length and feel of sticks until you have hit the ball with them; and you are advised to borrow some of various sorts from friends, since even if you could persuade a shop to let you have sticks on approval, you would dent their heads when you struck the ball, and have to pay for them anyway!

Later on, when you are more proficient, you should try out your sticks on a live pony; but at first you had better do this on a wooden horse, or else, if you are forced to select them in a shop, you must insist on being allowed to give each stick several full swings. Some firms provide a saddle on

EQUIPMENT

a trestle for this purpose; otherwise you can stand on a chair or table; but whichever it is to be, the full swing is most desirable.

Choose the stick that is pleasant to swing, and that gives you an impression that when you hit the ball the stick-head will be 'doing all the work'; even though it may not be the stick that felt best when you were standing on the ground, and shaking it in your hand.

LENGTH OF THE STICK

Sticks are made in different lengths, to suit the personal fancy of the player and the height of his pony. They are referred to by their length in inches, the commonest lengths lying between forty-eight and fifty-four. They are also to be had to the nearest half-inch.

On the question whether to play with a long stick or a short one there is apt to be a difference of opinion.

Some players use a stick of medium length, some use the shortest with which they can hit the ball, saying it is easiest to manage accurately; and some recommend the longest with which the off-side drive can be made, saying that this gives them a longer reach for badly placed shots, and enables them to take 'pulled backhanders' under the pony's tail with greater efficiency.

Since expert opinion is divided, and as it will be some time before you can make such shots, you cannot do better than take the middle course, and choose a stick with which you can comfortably make the ordinary off-side forehander, keeping the correct position (as illustrated in Plate IV facing page 34). If you are of average height, and play on an average-sized pony, this should be about a fifty-one.

If you begin to find that playing with such a stick is making you raise or drop your shoulders, or stoop unduly, it will be evident that you need a shorter or a longer one; but you are advised at any rate to start with one of medium length, for this will enable you to form a better judgment of what you need.

It is quite possible to learn striking with one stick, and perhaps a spare; and you will find it useful, when you come to play, that you should be able to use the same stick on every pony of reasonable height. You can learn to do this by adjusting the height of your shoulder at the top of your swing. But if you find that it interferes with the quality of your stroke, get a stick one inch longer, and one an inch shorter, than you have chosen to play with on the average-sized pony; and these should suit you on all ponies,

EQUIPMENT

from the biggest to the smallest (with the exception, of course, of smaller *breeds*, such as China ponies or Burmese Tats).

When you come to play in tournaments, you will need at least one spare stick of each size that you are using, to replace any that may break in the game. You will find it useful to mark your sticks of different lengths distinctively; and a simple and effective way to do this is to have a band of colour painted round the shaft near the stick-head, since a colour is far easier to distinguish quickly than any figure would be. If you go in for half-inch distinctions, a second and narrower band can be painted on the shaft above the main colour band. Your system of colouring is immaterial, but the following scheme is already used by a number of players: 54, yellow; 53, white; 52, blue; 51, red; 50, green; 49, grey; and 48, brown.

TYPES OF HANDLE

There are three principal types of handle, illustrated opposite page 18:

The O.H.K., or Rugby, shown in Plate IIa;

the Lloyd, or Racquet, shown in Plate IIb;

and the Parada, in Plate IIc.

The O.H.K., or Rugby, handle, which is usually flatter than the Lloyd, or Racquet, is the old standard type. By being broadened on the inner side of the shaft only (and not on either side equally, like the Lloyd, or Racquet), it has the advantage of making the stick practically prolong the line of the arm at contact, as in Plates IIIa and IIIc. For this reason it is the handle which used to be in more general use among polo-players.

The Parada handle has been specially designed for players that use the finger-grip illustrated in Plate III, and is recommended for them since it combines the advantage of being broadened out on the inner side only with that of having no rim at the end. The raised rim that you will notice round the head of the other handles was originally intended to prevent the stick from slipping through the hand; but this was in the days when it was assumed that the stick would be held in a 'palm-grip'; for the stick was then always held in the palm of the hand, like a tennis-racquet, with the end of the handle projecting through the hand. It is claimed by those who still use the palm-grip that it has the advantage of slightly added comfort and security at the top of the swing in a stroke; but

EQUIPMENT

this advantage is more than counterbalanced by the fact that in a palm-grip the stick does not, at the moment of impact, prolong the line of the arm so well as when held the other way, unless a cramped and awkward position is assumed. For this reason the finger-grip, is the one recommended.

With the finger-grip, however (illustrated in Plate III), the little finger is made to go over the rim at the end of the handle, and the stick no longer projects through the hand; and so the object of the raised rim has disappeared. In doing away with the rim itself, the Parada handle makes the position of the little finger far more comfortable, and obviates the danger of the stick's slipping through the hand by providing a notch which enables it to be held in a kind of pistol-grip.

This is the type of handle recommended to beginners. But should you decide to play with a Parada, you must realise that you will find yourself at a disadvantage if you become accustomed to the additional comfort of the pistol-grip and are suddenly forced to play with another type of handle. For this reason, you must either go to the expense of stocking up a sufficient number in advance, or else make sure that your Sports Dealer stocks Parada handles. If you don't think you can manage this, you had better keep to the standard O.H.K., or Rugby, which you will find obtainable wherever you may be.

Handles can be covered in soft white leather, smooth brown rubber, and red or black rubber (either rough or smooth). Cotton-wick is also used, and helps to absorb the sweat of the hand. In hot climates towelling is sometimes used for this purpose; but it is liable to fray and needs frequent replacing.

THE SLINGS

Nearly all sticks have a loop of tape, called the 'slings', which is intended to save you from being disarmed if your stick is hooked.

On most sticks the slings are at the *end* of the handle. There are two ways of adjusting them: you can either thrust your right hand through them and give the stick three or four turns so that the tape fits comfortably round the wrist, leaving you scope enough to catch hold of the handle, as shown in Plates IIIa and IIIb; or else you can put your thumb only through them and, passing them down the back of your hand, bring the stick upright inside your palm before catching hold of it as in Plates IIIc and IIId. Try both ways, and see which you prefer. You will find that

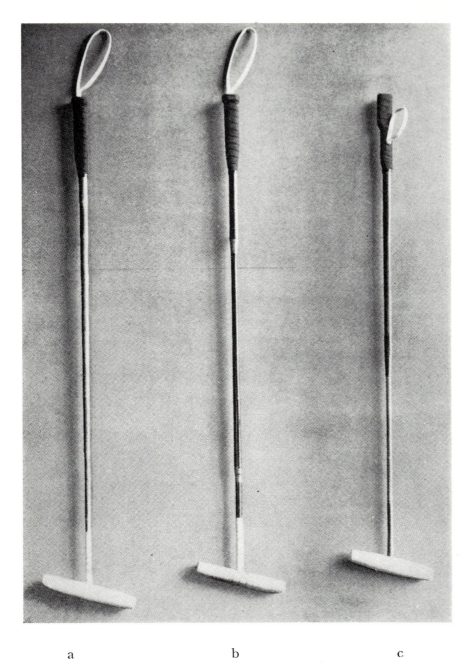

a b c

PLATE II *Types of Stick*

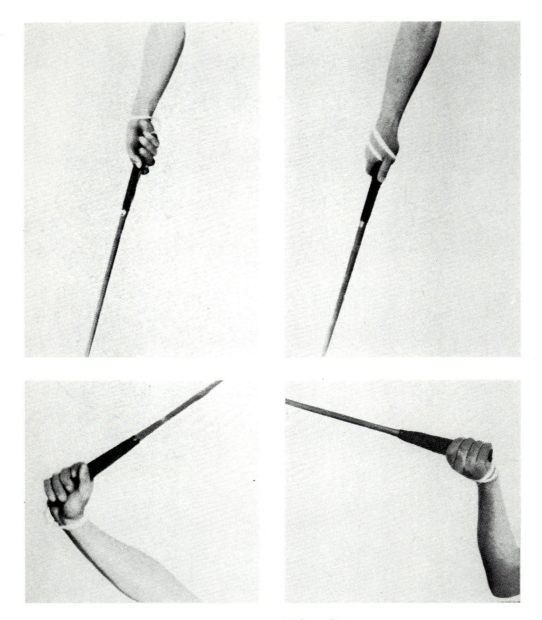

a
b PLATE III *The Grip* c
d

EQUIPMENT

the second way enables you to disengage the stick more easily and quickly, but if this way is to be comfortable you will need to fit the length of the slings more carefully.

The slings are sometimes put at the side of the handle as in Plate IIc. You will probably find them easier to adjust in this case, since you need only put your hand (or better, your first three fingers) through them. You might have some difficulty, however, in replacing these at short notice, particularly when abroad: so they are recommended to you with the same reservations as in the case of the Parada handle, the sling at the end being the article more generally available.

SHAPE, DIMENSIONS, AND WEIGHT OF THE HEAD

There are two principal shapes of head, with a circular cross-section:

> The cigar-shape;
> and the cylindrical.

Other shapes, such as the square and the Le Gallais, are old-fashioned, and are now rarely seen.

In the cigar-shaped head the bulk of the weight is in the centre, where the head hits the ball; whilst in the cylindrical head, the weight is evenly distributed.

In both sorts, the heel[1] can be cut away, to facilitate shots taken far out from the pony's side, or under his neck or tail. A further refinement, to facilitate shots taken very close to his side, is to cut away the toe as well, and slightly flatten the underside; the resulting shape being, in both the cigar-shaped and cylindrical heads, called a 'Jodhpur' head.

More drive is obtained from a cigar-shaped head, and when its cross-section is modified as explained below the drive will be still further increased.

Heads are measured by dimensions and weight.

The length of heads varies by half-inches from $8\frac{1}{2}$ to $9\frac{1}{2}$; and their diameter varies between $1\frac{5}{8}$ and $1\frac{13}{16}$ inches.

Their weight varies by quarter-ounces between 6 and $7\frac{1}{2}$ oz.

Obviously, the length, diameter, and weight of a head are to a certain extent interdependent; but if a heavy head of small diameter is required, for instance, the chief polo-stick manufacturers can usually provide this by cutting it from a denser part of the log than is usually the case.

---

[1] The heel is the inner end of the stick-head, and the toe the outer end.

EQUIPMENT

Some manufacturers give special names to their stick-heads, according to the diameter, or length; but it is simpler when ordering sticks to quote the dimensions required.

Plate IIa shows a $9\frac{1}{2}$-inch cigar-shaped small-diameter head, with the heel cut away. Plate IIb shows a 9-inch cylindrical Jodhpur head. Plate IIc shows an $8\frac{1}{2}$-inch cigar-shaped large-diameter head.

Large-diameter heads are stronger, since there is a greater volume of wood in proportion to the hole for the shaft; but small-diameter heads are better for lofting the ball, since they get further underneath it (compare Figures 3a and 3b).

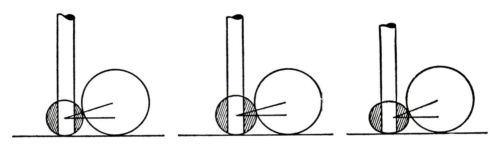

FIG. 3. CROSS-SECTIONS OF STICK-HEADS

a Small Diameter (Circular)   *b Large Diameter (Circular)*   *c R.N.P.A. (Elliptical)*

When the original manuscript of this book was being written in 1930 the comparison of the advantages and disadvantages of large and small diameter heads of circular cross-section given in the previous paragraph led to the conclusion that a head of elliptical cross-section would afford the advantages of both type of head whilst obviating both their disadvantages, provided the elliptical head was constructed as shown in Figure 3c.

Such a head was therefore constructed and christened the R.N.P.A. Head (after the Royal Naval Polo Association, which took out the patent on this head). It proved in practice to give greater loft, since its vertical diameter is less than that of a small diameter head (and this enables it to get well underneath the ball). But it also proved to give greater strength and both last longer and give greater drive, since its horizontal diameter is greater than that of a large diameter head, and consequently no bulk in this direction has to be sacrificed.

It's success was phenomenal, no less than 5,000 heads a year being sold by 1938 in Europe and U.S.A., and a comparably large but unrecorded

EQUIPMENT

number in India. The R.N.P.A. head is therefore strongly recommended to you and a good size and weight are 9½ inches and 6¾ ounces respectively.

MATERIALS FOR THE SHAFT OF THE STICK

Four principal kinds of cane are used in the Shafts of polo-sticks:
  Long-jointed tapered cane, shown in Plate IIa,
  Short-jointed tapered,
  Moonah Cane,
  Malacca, either natural, or smoked (shown in Plate IIb).

Often two canes are used, spliced together, the handle-end being usually of natural malacca, and the head-end of moonah, as shown in Plate IIc. Other variations are possible, the object being to produce a perfectly tapered stick with its 'whip' low down near the head.

In the table below, the qualities of the various canes have been assessed and 'marked' out of a maximum of ten. Marks have been given, in the case of resiliency, for the *potential* resiliency of the materials, since each can be obtained in varying degrees of whip as required. There are two or three distinct varieties of long-jointed cane, but they have been combined under one heading, as their qualities are similar.

TABLE I. SHAFTS

Quality	Long-jointed tapered	Short-jointed tapered	Natural Malacca	Smoked Malacca	Moonah	Spliced Malacca and Moonah
Drive	8	7	10	10	8	9
Balance	8	10	6	7	6	9
Durability	9	4	7	5	10	8
Retention of shape	7	7	7	10	9	8
Resiliency	9	8	8	9	6	8
Total	41	36	38	41	39	42

MATERIALS FOR THE HEAD OF THE STICK

Three principal kinds of wood are used in the Heads of polo-sticks:
  Sycamore;
  Ash;
  Bamboo, (which is sometimes bound with vellum and provides a fourth category).

EQUIPMENT

In the table below, the qualities of these are assessed and marked out of a maximum of ten, as in Table I.

TABLE II. HEADS

Quality	Sycamore	Ash	Bamboo	Vellum-covered Bamboo
Drive - - - -	10	8	7	7
Durability - - -	4	7	10	10
Imperviousness to wet -	10	9	8	4
Total - - - -	24	24	25	21

SELECTION OF MATERIALS FOR SHAFTS AND HEADS

Since there are six variations possible in the shafts of sticks, and four in the heads, there are obviously twenty-four possible combinations from which to choose your stick.

The tables show that each material is strong in certain qualities and weak in others. As your game improves and you discover what your needs are, you should be able, with the help of these tables, to strike a balance of qualities that will give you what you specially need without depriving you of anything essential to your stroke.

If you find, for instance, that you want to drive a longer ball, try a sycamore head on a malacca shaft: but be prepared for additional expense. If your wrist is particularly weak, or you have strained it, try a short-jointed tapered with a sycamore head, though this again will be expensive. You will find smoked malacca a good stiff cane, but brittle; whereas a bamboo head on moonah is both economical and reliable in match play.

These recommendations could be prolonged; but you can study the tables yourself, and work out for yourself a type of stick that will best meet your requirements. For the best all-round stick the object should be to avoid any serious defect rather than to go for one special quality. The combination of stick and head which scores the most marks is a spliced Malacca and Moonah with a Bamboo head. This is the one, in Plate IIc, which is recommended to you. If it is not obtainable, a long jointed tapered shaft is the next best alternative.

EQUIPMENT

THE STICK RECOMMENDED TO THE BEGINNER

To sum up, then, the advice given under various headings in the foregoing pages as to the kind of stick suitable to the beginner, you are recommended to choose the stick illustrated in Plate IIc (but with an R.N.P.A. head).

About fifty-one inches long.

Not too whippy (especially not near the handle), with a Parada handle with slings at the side.

With a spliced Malacca and Moonah shaft, and a $9\frac{1}{2}$ inch R.N.P.A. $6\frac{3}{4}$ oz. Bamboo head.

The total weight of the stick should be about $17\frac{1}{2}$ oz.

If this precise stick is not available then the next best alternatives are:

Handle: O.H.K. or Rugby.

Slings: at the end.

Shaft: long-jointed tapered.

Head: cigar shaped, small diameter, ash, with its heel cut away.

The alternative stick is shown in Plate IIa.

After a season's play, you may already find that you want to change your type of stick. Your wrist may have strengthened so that you feel you can do with a heavier head; and if you have become more supple you may wish to play with a rather shorter stick.

But whatever changes you effect should be made gradually.

THE CARE OF STICKS

When your sticks are not in use, keep them hung up by their slings, and not by their heads.

They should be kept out of the sun in hot weather, as dry heat softens the cane and affects its natural resiliency. This is particularly the case with tapered canes. The best cane for use in hot climates is smoked malacca, which is not affected by the heat.

If you want to straighten out a cane that has become bent, do so very gently: unnecessary force or overbending destroys its resiliency.

You are strongly advised to put india-rubber rings on your sticks, particularly on malacca and tapered canes, to protect the shaft when it is struck by a bouncing ball. Three rings weigh only one-eighth of an ounce.

EQUIPMENT

Bamboo heads should be painted (preferably white), to preserve them and to prevent them from absorbing moisture on a wet day and becoming sodden.

Be careful when oiling heads not to let oil get on to the binding or on to where the head is pegged-up. Never oil ash or bamboo heads, for this causes them to fray.

It has been found in very hot, dry climates that vellum-covered bamboo heads stand the heat better than uncovered ones.

SADDLERY

For a pony playing polo, the following is the minimum equipment that you will need:

SADDLE

The saddle should be fitted to your pony and care taken to see that it does not pinch him or press on his withers. Nor must it press upon his spine, and it should leave his shoulders free and unimpeded.

Don't buy a saddle with flaps cut well forward, as it will have been designed specially for riding with short stirrups, and will give you the wrong kind of seat for polo, where you will have to stand in the stirrups to strike the ball.

If you are buying a saddle abroad, it will probably pay you to look for second-hand ones by good English makers. On a good saddle, the maker's name will usually be found on the stirrup-leather bar.

BRIDLE

The fitting and choice of a bridle are very important, for they will make the whole difference to the way your pony goes.

Most ponies will go either in a double bridle or in a half-moon Pelham.

If studs are used instead of stitching, different bits can be used.

The bit must be fitted to the pony; if it is too wide across the mouth-piece, it is apt to become lop-sided, and will injure the bars of his mouth. When a bit is correctly fitted in a pony's mouth, it should hang touching the top of his lips, but not wrinkling them up. If it hangs too low he will learn to get his tongue over, whilst if it is too high he will be uncomfortable.

A good rough guide to fitting a curb-chain correctly is as follows: Hang one end on the off-side curb-hook; twist the chain *clockwise*, till it lies flat,

EQUIPMENT

and put the end link on the near-side hook, while holding your thumb-nail upwards; then put on the required link, this time with your thumb-nail turned down, having gripped the chain the same way both times. This should make the chain lie flat on the sides of the pony's mouth, touching the chin-groove when the bit and rein make a right-angle. It is most important when the chain is in position, that it should be lying flat and not twisted. If you find this difficult to do satisfactorily, from following the above description, get someone competent to show you how to do it.

Inspect the fitting of your bridle, and fit the curb-chain yourself, before getting up to play polo. Grooms are only human, and they will often make a mistake that can give your pony eight minutes of acute discomfort, and spoil your fun for a whole chukka.

You should also have a snaffle for your groom to exercise the pony in.

STANDING MARTINGALE

The Martingale should be just long enough, when fitted, to enable the pony to stop properly with its head up.

BOOTS

An addition to Hurlingham Polo Association Field Rule 4 (see page 125) makes the protection of ponies by boots or bandages compulsory. (This rule, however, is not included in the United States Polo Association rules.) You will need to have one or other for each of your pony's legs. They should not interfere with the action of his knee, but should amply protect his fetlock joint. Leather-covered boots are twice as expensive as felt ones, but they last three times as long.

TAIL BANDAGE

You will need a tail-bandage to prevent the pony's tail from catching on the polo-stick.

STABLE GEAR

The following is the minimum of gear that you will need for a stable of your own:

Dandy-brush, for removing caked mud and surface dirt. It should also be used for grooming the pony's tail, which must never be combed.

EQUIPMENT

Body-brush, for cleaning the coat and skin. The real grooming should be done with this.

Curry-comb, for rubbing the dirt off the brushes.

Scraper, for scraping the sweat off ponies immediately after playing.

Stable rubbers, (*i.e.* cloths), for drying the pony's coat. These can also be used, rolled up, in place of a wisp.

Wisp, made of straw or hay, for massaging the pony's body. It should be brought down with a bang onto the skin, in the direction of the growth of the hair, and dragged down.

Hoof-pick, for cleaning out the foot.

Sponge, for cleaning the eyes, nose and dock (in that order for obvious reasons). Separate sponges are preferable, but not essential.

Measure, for measuring out feeds accurately.

A rug and a blanket, to put over the pony.

Roller (*i.e.* a padded surcingle for keeping the rug in place).

Head collar, and a rope.

A set of stable bandages, for veterinary purposes.

A bottle of disinfectant, iodine, and a tin of anti-phlogistine.

Water bucket.

DRESS

Spurs, which you are likely to want as you become more proficient, must be blunt, as the Field Rules forbid the use of sharp spurs.

General Rule 9 makes a protected polo helmet or cap, which must be worn with a chin strap, obligatory. Get one with a plain white puggaree unless you are entitled to a service, regimental or club puggaree. (The Royal Navy wear a blue puggaree or an all blue polo cap.)

It is quite customary for beginners to play in brown breeches, so you need not go to the expense of getting a pair of white ones until later. Few people will object to your playing your first game in black boots if they are all you have; but later on, when you start 'riding-off' you should invest in brown boots, so that no blacking will be left on your opponents' breeches.

Any sort of short-sleeved shirt or jersey will do to begin with; later you should get a white polo-vest and a coloured one. The international teams and most other players wear thin woollen or cotton vests with short sleeves and an open neck (see Frontispiece).

Wear either thin drawers reaching below the knees, or thin stockings reaching above them; for if you wear nothing between your breeches and

EQUIPMENT

your skin, you will find that your legs chafe on the inside of your knees. This is due to the unusual amount of movement in the saddle at polo, and affects even good riders. If you find that your legs chafe all the same, lubricate the affected part by rubbing it with a dampened piece of soap, or vaseline, or sprinkle it liberally with powder.

The easiest polo whip to use is one at least 40 inches long, as it can be applied from the left hand across your left leg.

POLO-PIT, AND WOODEN HORSE

The best way to start learning to strike is from the back of a wooden horse in a polo-pit.

Many clubs in England have a polo-pit; and in many places abroad you will also find one.

In its simplest form, it consists of a pit dug in the ground, with a flat centre on which is placed a wooden horse carrying a saddle.

Figure 4 shows a rather more elaborate form of pit, equipped with a roof and electric light, which make practising possible in wet weather and on winter evenings. The figure gives the principal dimensions of a specimen pit; but not the constructional details, which can be supplied by any builder. Figure 4a is the centre-section of the end elevation; Figure 4b, the centre-section of the side elevation; Figure 4c, the end elevation from the exterior; and Figure 4d the plan-view of the interior.

This pit consists of a wooden framework, round which a wire netting is stretched on all four sides. It supports a corrugated-iron pent-house roof. Inside this structure, the flooring slopes downwards to a flat, central platform, on which the wooden horse stands. There is a door in one side, rather behind and to the right of the horse.

The wire netting is sloped inwards and then out again, at each end, as shown in Figure 4b, in order to prevent the ball from climbing the wire when it is hit hard; and there is a rather similar projection of wire along each side, for the same reason. The front of the wire-netting that slopes inwards at the ends should be of double thickness, to withstand hard-driven shots; and sacking can be hung loosely over it, to break the force of the ball.

When the ball is hit, it travels up the slope, is stopped by the net, and rolls down again towards the striker, giving him practice, while mounted on a stationary horse, at hitting a moving ball. It is of course perfectly possible to learn from the back of a live pony, but it is more difficult; and your progress will not be so fast as if you can accustom yourself to the idea

EQUIPMENT

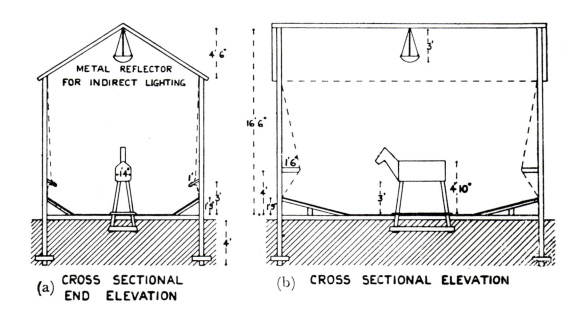
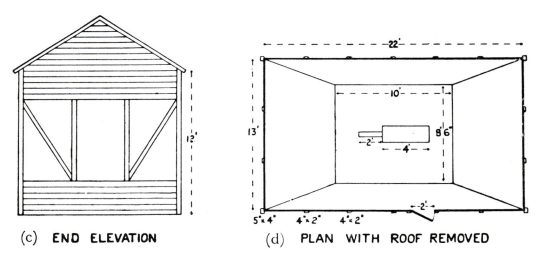

FIG. 4. DETAILS FOR A POLO-PIT

EQUIPMENT

of the strokes without having to bother about controlling your mount.

If you cannot have access to a properly built pit, you will find it well worth your while to run-up a makeshift wooden horse to practise from. This can be done quite easily and inexpensively if you are not too ambitious.

FIG. 5. THE WOODEN HORSE

Figure 5 shows a rough stand 58 inches high[1] made of wooden battens fixed horizontally to a frame which is securely bolted to four wooden legs. A board is fixed to project about two feet from the top of the stand, as shown in the figure; and to this the reins should be tied. A good plan is to tie these on with several strands of cotton so that each time you jerk your 'horse' in the mouth while striking the ball, you will have the trouble of tying them on again.

A rough stand of this sort is all that you will need for practising the correct 'swing' in each kind of stroke; it can be also used for learning the actual hitting if you can't get to a pit, but in this case the horse will have to be set up either in a large, open space where the ball can do no damage, or else it must be surrounded with a net at a reasonable distance. This latter alternative is the most practical; but both proceedings are, of course, more cumbersome than a pit since you will either be able to practise hitting only

[1] A 15-hand pony stands 5 feet high only when measured at the withers, so he is usually about 2 inches lower than this under the saddle.

EQUIPMENT

at a stationary ball, or else you will have to find someone to bowl the ball to you from behind cover.

In the following instructions on Striking the ball, you will be assumed to have access to a pit, or to a makeshift arrangement. The procedure to adopt if nothing of this kind is available to you will be found on page 41, under the section on 'Hitting when Mounted'.

CHAPTER THREE

STRIKING

You are advised not to read this chapter and try to assimilate it at one sitting, but to take the points one at a time, trying over the various shots with a stick in your hand, so that you can form some idea of them before you start learning them seriously.

The strokes will be set out 'by numbers', and in as great detail as you will need, as a beginner; and you will find them introduced in the order in which it is suggested that you should learn them, both on account of their comparative difficulty and because of their usefulness to you as you begin to take part in the game.

Concentrate on one stroke at a time, and don't pass on to the next until you have reached a certain proficiency in it.

THE FOUR FUNDAMENTAL STROKES

There are four fundamental strokes in polo: the forward stroke on each side of the pony, and the backward stroke on each side. They are known as:

> The off-side forehander;
> the off-side backhander;
> the near-side forehander;
> and the near-side backhander.

With three subdivisions each:

> The drive;
> the pull;
> and the cut;

they comprise all the strokes in the game, with the exception of a few 'fancy' shots, which you can develop later, but with which, as a beginner, you will not need to concern yourself.

Before you can expect to play in a tournament, however, you will have to be reasonably proficient in the twelve strokes mentioned.

Figure 6 shows the four fundamental strokes, with their subdivisions.

The straight shot, in each case, is called the *drive*.

The *pull*, which crosses the line of advance, and the *cut*, which is made

STRIKING

at an angle away from it, are both intentional modifications of direction; and are not to be confused with similar *un*intentional deviations from the straight shot (in golf, for instance). The golfer can have no reason for not aiming straight, since he can easily alter the direction of his stance; but the polo-player can only change the direction of his brace (see next page) by changing that of his pony. Since he will often have no opportunity to do this, it is essential that he should know how to alter the direction of his shot without having to alter his own direction.

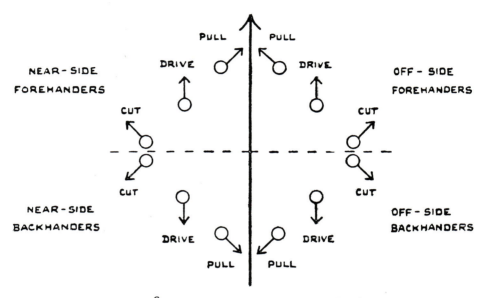

FIG. 6. THE TWELVE PRINCIPAL STROKES

But the normal application of each of the fundamental strokes is the drive. As a matter of fact, the swing remains the same, broadly speaking, in the cut and pulled shots as in the straight drive, until the extreme positions are reached in which the pony's body or legs would interfere with the stroke. There are, of course, certain modifications to be made in the plane of the swing; but you will find the instructions for cutting and pulling quite simple when you have thoroughly mastered the drive in each stroke.

THE REST POSITION

In the sections describing the strokes, you will in every case be assumed to start them from the rest position, since this is the position from which you will usually start your strokes in the game.

STRIKING

At the halt the usual rest position is as shown in the frontispiece of this book; but in the following pages the term will refer to the position in which your stick will be held in the game when it is not in use.

Hold the stick lightly in a vertically upright position, as shown in Figure 2 on page 12, with the hand held low, almost resting on the right knee. Don't grip it tight, for the position must be a comfortable one, and must put no strain on the muscles of your wrist and forearm. Try to avoid tilting the stick forward at an angle when you ride, for the weight of the stick-head, if you do so, will strain your muscles, and you will find that your wrist aches after the game.

THE BRACE

The brace is the name for the correct position in the saddle when you are taking your shot. It corresponds to the stance in golf, and is equally important.

You cannot expect to hit hard and accurately when sitting down, for you will have to use your body as well as your arm in making your stroke.

The correct brace is illustrated in Plates IV to VII, overleaf, and in Plates VIIIc, IXc and Xc following page 57.

To achieve the brace, rise in the stirrups and put your full weight on them, maintaining the position by gripping hard with your knees and thighs.

Practise this by rising in the stirrups and holding the correct position for a few moments, while you twist your body freely from the hips. When you come to take shots in this position, you will find in actual practice that you lean forward when hitting forward, and that you may even lean slightly back when hitting back.

THE GRIP OF THE STICK

There are two distinct grips in polo: the normal grip, and the reverse grip.

These used to be known as the forehand and backhand grips respectively. But the so-called 'forehand' grip is used in near-side *backhand* shots as well as in off-side forehand shots, whilst the 'backhand' grip is used in near-side *forehand* shots as well as in off-side backhand shots. Consequently, the use of the terms forehand and backhand as applied to a grip can lead to endless confusion; and for this reason the expressions 'normal' and 'reverse' have come to be used in their place.

STRIKING

The *normal* grip is illustrated in Plate IIIa (facing page 19).

You will see that this is a finger-grip, and that the butt-end of the handle does not project through the hand. In this way the stick is made to prolong as much as possible the line of the arm, at the moment of impact with the ball.

The *reverse* grip is illustrated in Plate IIIc.

You will see that this is also a finger-grip.

To change from the normal into the reverse grip, twist the stick $\frac{1}{4}$ turn clockwise, so that your thumb falls naturally down the flat of the handle.

A few players use the normal grip for all shots, and claim that this enables them to take a shot more quickly in the (rare) case of its having to be taken suddenly on the unexpected side of the pony. But it is generally considered that the stick is not so easy to control as when the grips are both used; so you are strongly advised to learn and practise them both.

THE IDEAL STROKE

The success of your stroke will depend entirely on how near you come to an ideal combination of three factors: you should aim at making the correct swing, in the correct plane, and at the correct time.

Timing, and the adjustment of the plane of your swing, are things you will learn when you are swinging at the ball.

First of all, however, long before there can be any question of your trying to hit a ball, you will have to learn to make the correct swing.

THE SWING

The first thing you must realise is the precise function of the swing: the stick is swung so that the stick-head may gather momentum and the shaft may guide it to the ball. The head will then expend most of its energy in driving the ball, and the remainder in the course of the 'follow-through'.

Don't think that by forcing strength through to the head of the stick you will succeed in hitting a longer ball. Brute force in your swing will be useless, unless it be scientifically applied; and the governing factor in long hitting, assuming your timing to be correct, will be the speed that you impart to the head of the stick.

The theory of the swing is illustrated in Figures 8, 9, 10 and 11 on pages 38, 43, 47 and 49. In these diagrams of the swings of the four fundamental strokes, the positions shown trace the path of the stick and forearm from the

a　　PLATE IV　*The Off-side Forehander*　　b

a　　PLATE V　*The Off-side Backhander*　　b

a   PLATE VI *The Near-side Forehander*   b

a   PLATE VII *The Near-side Backhander*   b

STRIKING

top of the swing until the position of contact with the ball is reached. The positions are equally spaced, with regard to time, in each diagram, having been obtained from enlargements of a slow-motion film. Plates IV to VII, help to illustrate the swing. They have been obtained by superimposing a photograph of the striker when he is at the top of his swing, on to a photograph taken when he is making contact with the ball.

You will see that the stick, pivoting about the wrist, turns through a considerably greater angle than the arm and shoulder. But, once the swing is established, the arm turns through almost equal angles (which shows, incidentally, that the swing is smooth and regular); whilst the stick-head turns through increasingly greater ones. The stick, in other words, is gradually gathering speed: until, at the position of contact, when it reaches its greatest momentum, it has caught up the arm and shoulder and is in one straight line with them.

By swinging as in Figures 8 to 11, you will be imparting far greater speed to the stick-head than if your arm and the stick had been in a straight line at the top of your swing; since it is by being turned through a far greater angle in the same amount of time that the stick will have acquired greater momentum.

It is this *momentum* that puts length into the drive.

Think for a moment of the stick-head as if it were a lead weight on a line: such as the leadsman uses in a ship, to take soundings. If the lead acquired momentum, and a polo-ball were placed in position, it is obvious that you could make the ball travel as if you had made a similar shot with a polo-stick. But, without a solid shaft to connect you with the lead, it would have been impossible for you to force the pace unevenly. As a matter of fact, few low-handicapped players can have failed to surprise themselves, when swinging easily with the intention of making a short pass, on finding that the ball has travelled further than they meant it to, because they had omitted all misdirected force.

The fact that certain materials, when used in the shaft of the stick, enable a longer ball to be driven is due to their resiliency, and does not affect the general truth of this statement.

Beginners are seldom content to feel that the head of the stick is 'doing all the work', and that its momentum will bring their hand along with it. Through forcing the hand ahead of the stick at the position of contact, they will often 'top' the ball, as shown in Figure 7 (unless they have committed the further fault of dropping the shoulder).

Although the action of the wrist plays an important part in striking, it

STRIKING

should be allowed to work without any conscious 'snap' that could destroy the smoothness of the swing. During the whole of the swing the wrist will be straightening out, and its action in doing this should be smooth with no extra effort just before the contact position is reached. If the swing has been correctly made, the rate at which the stick has gained on the arm will bring them into one straight line at the moment of contact with the ball.

The foregoing remarks apply, of course, to the swing for a full stroke, and not to short 'flick' shots, which are made largely by means of wrist work.

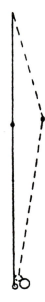

FIG. 7. TOPPING THE BALL THROUGH PRESSING

Make up your mind to learn the swing gradually and scientifically, so that by the time you come to apply it to the ball there will be no tendency to hurry or 'press', and a correct style will be second nature to you.

LEARNING THE SWING, 'BY NUMBERS'

The swing for each of the four fundamental strokes can be learnt in three motions, by numbers, as follows:

One, the preparatory;
Two, the top of the swing;
Three, the swing itself (which includes the follow-through).

STRIKING

Start learning these by making them with a slight pause between consecutive motions. Don't try to learn the swing of more than one stroke at a time. Confine yourself first of all to the off-side forehander. Not only is it the easiest to learn, but it is the stroke you will want to use more than any other when you begin to play.

Get a friend to read over the following instructions to you in the pit and compare your positions with those in the Plates.

THE OFF-SIDE FOREHAND SWING

Starting from the rest position, the three motions of the off-side forehand swing are as follows:

One. Tighten your grip on the stick, so that the handle comes into the correct *normal* grip. The head of the stick should be tilted forward at an angle of about 45 degrees and slightly to the left, the heel being pointed forward and down, as shown in Figure 5 on page 29, and Plate VIIIa.

Two. Rising in the stirrups to the correct brace, carry your right hand back and upwards (see Plate Xa), extending the arm to the fullest possible extent, so that the hand comes to rest considerably above the level of the top of your head (see Plates IV, IXa and Xb).

As the hand comes back, point your left shoulder at the ball, by twisting your body to the right, from the hips, and leaning well over to the right, as shown in Plates IVa and IXa. When you are at the top of your swing, your right shoulder should be turned so far back that it is in line with your extended arm, as shown in Plates IVb, VIIIb, IXa and Xb.

The stick-head should be left pointing forward as the hand comes back, so that the stick ends up tilted forward and to the left, about 35 degrees above the horizontal, and has its toe pointing forward and down, as shown in Plate VIIIb. Some players bring it even further down (Plate IXa); whilst others do not bring it down so far (Plate Xb); but you are advised to learn the swing with the stick in the medium position (about 35 degrees) at the top.

The top of your swing is most important (Plates IIIb, facing page 19, and IV). Keep your hand well above the level of the top of your head, so that the head of the stick will have sufficient space in which to gather speed.

Practise getting up to the top of your swing smoothly, and without hurrying, so that the transition from the preparatory position to the swing itself may be as rhythmical as possible.

Three. Plates IXb and Xc show the swing in progress. Begin by

STRIKING

rotating your shoulders, keeping your head stationary, so that it acts as a pivot. The fore and upper arm should be kept in one straight line with the shoulders during the swing. This movement will start the head of the stick swinging backwards, as shown in Figure 8.

You should be able to feel the outward pull exerted by the centrifugal force on the stick-head.

At the contact-position, shoulder, arm, and stick should be in one straight line, as shown in Figure 8 and in Plates IVb and Xd.

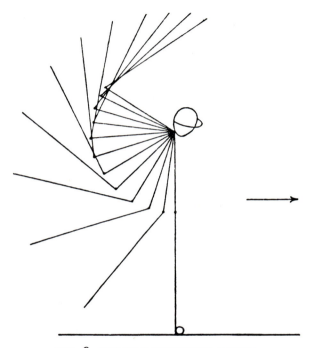

FIG. 8. OFF-SIDE FOREHAND SWING

When the contact-position is passed, do not neglect the follow-through. If you make your swing correctly, and continue to rotate the shoulders, you will find that the stick follows through as in Plates VIIIf and Xf. It is, of course, immaterial when once you have hit the ball, whether you follow through or not; but, unfortunately, if you form the habit of checking your follow-through, your subconscious wish to do so will have its effect just *before* you hit the ball, and will ruin your swing. Make sure that the follow-through takes its natural course.

A common fault is to start the swing with the head and shoulders too high. In this case you will have to drop your head and shoulders during the

STRIKING

last and most critical part of your swing to avoid topping the ball. This will spoil the equilibrium of your swing and tend to produce inaccurate hitting. The remedy, of course, is to bend your head and shoulders lower when leaning out to get into the correct position for the top of the swing.

The correct position can best be verified by first getting into the contact position and then slowly lifting the stick-head backwards, whilst pivoting the shoulders about the head in the reverse direction until the position of the top of the swing is reached. This position should then be memorised. It can immediately be checked by carrying out the normal swing and observing whether the stick-head just grazes the ground without having to drop or raise the head.

When you have successfully made the swing by numbers, do it in one even motion, pausing only for a moment at the top and coming back each time to the rest position.

LEARNING TO HIT OFF-SIDE FOREHANDERS

When you are satisfied with your swing, start hitting at a stationary ball, and practising the off-side forehand *stroke*.

It is now that the second element of your stroke will be introduced: the adjustment of the plane of your swing.

In any stroke you make at polo, the head of the stick should travel in a plane inclined at the same slight angle from the vertical as that at which the stick is tilted from the vertical when the contact-position is reached; and this plane should cut the ground in the direction of aim. Any divergence from this will affect the direction, as well as the style, of your stroke. The plane of the swing is shown clearly in Plate IVa, where the stick in its two positions lies in exactly the same plane.

If you have gripped the stick correctly and have been making the correct swing, you will have realised that you are to hit the ball 'broad-side on' with the stick-head (and not with its toe or heel, as if you were using a croquet-mallet!), and that the length of the head must be at a right-angle, at the moment of impact, to the direction in which you intend to strike.

Place the ball in line with the point of your right shoulder when you are in the contact-position in a correctly made swing (Plate IVb) and slightly out to your right (Plate IVa).[1]

---

[1] On page 52, in the section on Loft and Length, an alternative position, six inches in front of this, is recommended. A satisfactory shot can be taken with the ball anywhere between these two positions. This applies to both the forehand strokes.

STRIKING

Begin by taking a half-shot: that is to say, strike the ball by drawing the stick-head back three or four feet and swinging it forward lightly.

As soon as you feel fairly confident of hitting the ball clean with the centre of the stick-head, in a direction straight ahead, start taking a full shot at the ball.

Place the ball as before, and hit it quite gently, doing your swing by numbers, with a slight pause between consecutive motions, as when you first started to learn it. After doing this a few times, you will probably find that you can succeed in hitting the ball, taking a full shot in quick time.

Keep your Eye on the Ball.

However correctly you make your swing, it will not be in the correct plane unless you keep your eye on the ball from the moment of starting your stroke until you have absolutely finished it.

Make a point of bending your head well down. This will make you keep your eye on the ball, and will enable you in the game, not to see your opponent, and so not to be intimidated by him into pulling off the line of the ball when you are in legitimate possession. (Field Rule 16.)

When you can satisfactorily hit a stationary ball with a full swing in quick time, begin to practise on a moving ball.

It is now that the third element of your stroke will be introduced: that of timing your swing.

The timing of your swing is effected by your decision to start the second motion. As the ball approaches you, come into the preparatory position, and the moment you decide to strike, carry your hand back and rise in the stirrups.

If you watch carefully, you will see that good players, if they follow the method of striking recommended here, automatically adjust their timing, if they should have occasion to do so, by an almost imperceptible pause or acceleration at the top of the swing. Practise adjusting your timing in this way, in case (owing, for instance, to the ball's hitting a rough place and slowing up) you should have to do so when you are playing.

Swing early rather than late; for if you should have to pause, you can easily pause a moment longer, whilst if you should have to accelerate you will do so all the better for being up early.

Practise by tapping the ball up the slope of the pit, so that it rolls back within convenient hitting-distance. Don't hit wildly at it whenever it is within range, but tap it up the slope again properly before every shot you take.

After the first few times you need not come back each time into the rest

STRIKING

position; for in the game you will find that you come into the suitable preparatory position for your shot several seconds beforehand.

Don't overtire your wrist, thumb, and forearm. The muscles take some time to develop, and will be injured if they are overstrained.

Beware, too, of blisters: a glove or mitten on your right hand will reduce your chances of developing them.

When you are satisfied with your shots in the pit, start learning to take them mounted.

You were told in the preceding chapter how to put up a makeshift stand if no polo-pit is available. Failing this, you can always sit astride a balustrade to learn swinging, or on top of a wall; and in the last resort you can stand with your legs apart and swing with a walking-stick. But you should in no case try to learn your swing on a live animal.

You will have to learn to strike the ball, however, from a live pony, if there is no polo-pit available; and in this case you will do well to follow the plan outlined below, though it will mean, of course, that you have to spend considerably more time on each preliminary step than would otherwise have been the case.

Anyway, it will be assumed in the following remarks that you have already learnt the swing, and are satisfied that you can do it correctly.

HITTING WHEN MOUNTED

First of all, try and find a really quiet old polo-pony, so that you can concentrate on your hitting without having to worry about your mount.

The pony will need 'boots' on his forelegs to protect them from misdirected hits, for you will find that the legs of a moving pony get in your way more than you may have anticipated when you were practising on a wooden horse.

Begin by riding at a canter, and practising the off-side forehand swing without a ball: by numbers, at first, so as to accustom yourself to doing it while in motion.

Start hitting the ball with a half-shot, at a walk.

Then do the full shot, at a walk.

Then do the half-shot at the canter, and finally the full shot at the canter.

Have several balls lying about the practice-ground, so that you won't have to pull up and turn if you miss the ball.

Don't try to take a shot at the gallop until you are proficient in taking

STRIKING

it at the canter, as the timing is far more difficult. But you must practise taking shots at the gallop as soon as you feel that you can, for it will be essential that you should be able to do this before you can think of taking part in tournament polo.

You will notice that as you increase your pace you have to start your stroke further away from the ball, in order to make contact with it in the correct position. A good tip is to try and take the ball a foot or two in front of the point of your shoulder, as this will usually result in timing your shot correctly. The explanation of this, of course, is not that you actually take the ball two feet in front, but that if you had not made the necessary allowance you would have taken it much too far back. This allowance is not one that definite instructions can be given for, but must depend on the judgment you yourself come to develop in the course of playing.

Don't keep your pony at a full gallop for more than a few minutes each day, for this will be nearly as great a strain on him as playing in a game.

Practise hitting a moving ball, too, by tapping it on ahead and taking a full shot at it as you overtake it.

Don't neglect to practise direction.

The best way to do this is to aim at a goal; and most practice-grounds have at least two sets of goal-posts up for this purpose. Excellent practice, however, can be had by hitting two balls alternately past one another. In any case, always aim at something, even if only at a tuft of grass or a tree in the distance.

Don't let aiming at something make you take your eye off the ball. Look at your target and mentally register its direction, before you begin your stroke. If you don't train yourself to do this, you will fail to get your eye back on the ball in time, when you come to play, and will make an 'air-shot' whenever you shoot at goal!

While you are practising the off-side forehander mounted, and correcting in the pit any faults that may develop on the practice-ground, you should also be learning the next fundamental stroke in the pit.

THE OFF-SIDE BACKHAND SWING

Starting from the rest position, the three motions of the off-side backhand swing are as follows:

One. Tighten your grip on the stick, giving it a quarter of a turn to the right, as you do so: this will bring the handle into the correct position for the *reverse* grip (see Plate IIIc). The head of the stick should be tilted forward

STRIKING

at an angle of about 45 degrees, but should be at right angles to the direction of hitting and should have its toe pointing to the right.

Two. Rising in the stirrups to the correct brace, carry the right hand across your chest, so that the head of the stick drops over your left shoulder until it is about 20 degrees above the horizontal, and the hand comes to rest above the level of the top of your head. As your hand comes back, point

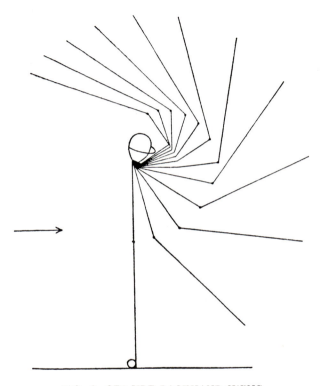

FIG. 9. OFF-SIDE BACKHAND SWING

your right shoulder forward and down at the ball, and lean your body over to the right.

This position can be studied in Plate V.

Three. Begin the swing as in the off-side forehander by rotating the shoulders about the head, which acts as a pivot (see Plate XXIb). This movement will start the stick-head moving forward and up as indicated in Figure 9.

Throw your hand *well forward*: the sooner your elbow straightens out, the greater the speed that will be imparted to the stick-head. At the contact

STRIKING

position your shoulder, arm and stick must be in one straight line as shown in Figure 9 and Plate Vb.

When the contact position has been passed and the ball has been struck, on no account neglect the follow-through; to achieve this, the body must continue to rotate after the ball has been struck, until finally the right arm and shoulder are pointing over the pony's off-quarter as shown in Plate XXId.

In theory it would be best if the head could be bent down far enough at the top of the swing to act as a true pivot, which would not be displaced with reference to the saddle (*i.e.* the datum which has been taken for the photographs). In practice this would restrict the rotation of the body at the top of the swing and prevent the hand from being brought sufficiently high above the head to obtain a really full swing. A slight outward and downward movement of the head must therefore be accepted in this stroke, as shown in Plate V.

ALTERNATIVE METHODS. Another way of doing this stroke is illustrated in Plates XIa to XIf, which show the swing being made on the right side of the body instead of across it. This method, sometimes known as the 'hammer stroke', prevents proper use being made of the body and makes it difficult to follow-through properly except by bending forward almost double, as shown in Plate XIf. (But if you consider, in the light of this illustration, to what lengths a first-class player will go to make a proper follow-through, even when it is most uncomfortable to do so, you should be convinced of how important it is not to neglect it.)

There is a third variation, which also uses a swing made completely on the right side of the body, the stick being swung through one and a half circles before it makes contact with the ball. It is generally known as the 'circular wind-up'. This stroke, also, receives no assistance from the body. and the circular wind-up is used to impart to the stick-head that speed which is normally induced by the rotation of the shoulders. This method has the disadvantage of greatly increasing the risk of having the stick hooked, and adding to the difficulty of timing an unexpected shot.

But the first method, across the body, is recommended to you, since it not only has the prettiest style, but also enables full use of the body to be made without discomfort.

LEARNING TO HIT OFF-SIDE BACKHANDERS

Once you are satisfied with your off-side backhand swing, done in quick time, start hitting at a stationary ball in the pit.

STRIKING

Place the ball in line with the point of your right shoulder when you are in the contact-position in a correctly made swing (Plate Vb)[1] and slightly out to your right (Plate Va).

Begin by taking a half-shot; unless practising the off-side forehander has given you sufficient control of the stick to enable you to omit this, in which case start on the full shot at once.

As soon as you are satisfied with your shots in the pit, begin hitting backhanders at a stationary ball, mounted. Follow the same scheme as for hitting forehanders mounted.

When you practise the off-side strokes on the practice-ground, don't alternate them, at first. Spend half your practice-time on one shot, and then half on the next.

When you are more or less confident of both your off-side shots, at the canter (or, preferably, at the gallop), you can start playing polo in club-chukkas.

STARTING TO PLAY

You will realise as soon as you begin to play that you will now have to start timing your shots rather differently from the way you timed them on the practice-ground.

When hitting a ball you were overtaking, you always had plenty of time for making your stroke, since the difference was never very great between your own speed and the speed of the ball. Now, however, you will also have to hit a ball travelling towards you; and your timing will have to be far more accurate than before, since the speed of the ball will have to be added to your own speed, and this will greatly reduce the time during which the ball is in position for striking.

In your first two or three months of play, you should spend more time practising than playing. But later you will, of course, come to play much more than you practise, and you may even be tempted to neglect practising at all. There are, to be sure, players that give up practising when they attain a certain degree of proficiency, but their handicap seldom increases after this; and it is certain that no high-handicap player manages to maintain his standard of play without devoting considerable time to practising.

Don't neglect your horsemanship.

---

[1] On page 52, in the section on Loft and Length an alternative position, six inches behind this, is recommended. A satisfactory shot can be taken with the ball anywhere between these two positions. This applies to both the backhand strokes.

STRIKING

Don't think you can now concentrate on your striking, and forget to practise what is almost as important in the game. Perhaps it would be excessive to say that riding is 'more than half the battle' in striking; but it is certainly true that the finest stroke done in the finest style will not do you much good, if your horsemanship is not equal to getting you to the right place to make it in!

When you have played a few times, start learning the near-side strokes.

Take one stroke at a time, and do as you did in learning the off-side ones: always be learning one stroke in the pit while you are practising the ones already learnt, on the ground; and remember to correct in the pit all faults that develop in playing.

THE NEAR-SIDE FOREHAND STROKE

Starting from the rest-position, the three motions of the near-side forehand swing are as follows:

One. Tighten your grip on the stick, so that the handle is brought into the correct position for the *reverse* grip, tilting the stick-head forward as before at an angle of about 45 degrees, but this time to the *left* of the pony's head, so as to facilitate the next motion.

Two. Rising in the stirrups to the correct brace, carry your right hand well over to the left side until it is level with your left cheek, but well beyond it (Plate VIa); and in front of it (Plate VIb). As the hand comes over, keep your right elbow bent (as shown in these two Plates), and, leaning well out, turn your body as far to the left as you can without shifting the position of your bridle-hand. Your right shoulder should now be pointing at the ball, as in Plate XIVb.

Be sure to bring your right shoulder well over, or you will cramp the movement of your right hand and cause it to rotate about the elbow instead of about the shoulder.

The correct grip and position of the stick at the top of the swing are shown in Plate IIId, facing page 19. The toe of the stick-head should be pointing forward and down (at about 15 degrees above the horizontal), the thumb being on the inner side of the handle.

Three. The beginning of the swing is illustrated in Plates XIVb, XVa, XVIa.

Begin by carrying your right hand slightly upwards and well back. This movement will start the stick-head swinging backwards, as shown in Figure 10.

STRIKING

Continue the backward movement of the hand as far as possible. The figure will illustrate how important this is, for otherwise a good rotary movement of the hand about the shoulder will not be set up. Provided that your stroke is properly timed, no factor contributes more to length in this stroke (since you cannot rotate your body), than the extent to which you succeed in bringing back your hand.

Plate VI reveals a large lateral displacement of the head. If the head were bent down, at the top of the swing, to the position it will occupy at the

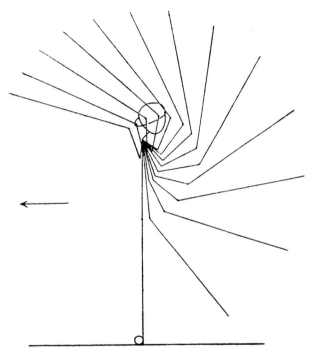

FIG. 10. NEAR-SIDE FOREHAND SWING

moment of contact, either the neck would get in the way of the swing (see Plate VIa) or the plane of the swing would have to be utterly destroyed to allow it to pass clear of the head. As the body is not rotated in this stroke, and the head does not have to act as a pivot, there is no objection to this movement of the head during the swing. The pivot in this stroke is the right shoulder, but even this has to move slightly to allow the arm and stick to clear the head. In practice, a compromise is reached in which the shoulder is kept in and the plane of the swing is very slightly displaced outwards until

STRIKING

the stick has cleared the head. This analysis sounds complicated but in fact the swing is not difficult to achieve with a little practice.

The Stroke. Before placing the ball for hitting near-side forehanders, look at Plate XVd, and compare it with Plate IXd.

In both cases the ball should be placed in line with the point of your shoulder when you are in the correct contact-position. But you will notice that, as in the near-side shot your shoulders will be turned round parallel to the pony, the point of your shoulder will come half-your-shoulder's width in front of the contact-position in the similar off-side shot.

THE NEAR-SIDE BACKHAND STROKE

Starting from the rest-position, the three motions of the near-side backhand swing are as follows:

One. Tighten your grip on the stick as for the off-side forehander, and use the *normal* grip.

Two. Rising in the stirrups to the correct brace, raise your right arm well above your head, extending it to the fullest possible extent and allowing the stick-head to drop back, until it is at about 20 degrees above the horizontal, as shown in Figure 11. The toe of the stick-head should be pointing backwards and down, as shown in Plate VIIb.

Point your left shoulder down and slightly forward at the ball, as in Plates XVIIIa and XVIIIb: the former actually shows the transition stage between the preparatory position and the top of the swing.

Three. Begin the swing by rotating the shoulders. This starts the stick-head travelling forward and upward as shown in Figure 11. It is important to keep your elbow straight from the top of the swing, so that the stick-head shall describe the largest possible circle and thus gain the greatest possible speed. Your arm and stick should, as usual, be in one straight line at the contact position as shown in Plate VIIb. You must lean well out and turn well to the left, as shown in Plate VIIa, to avoid catching your right arm against your left elbow.

In theory the head should not be displaced in this stroke, as it should act as a pivot for the shoulders. Plate VIIa makes it clear that to achieve this the neck would have to be bent sideways at the top of the swing until the head was very nearly horizontal. This position, besides being uncomfortable, would interfere with your ability to keep your eye properly on the ball. In practice, therefore, lean over only as far as you comfortably can, while keeping your head upright at the top of the swing and accept the fact that

STRIKING

you will have to drop your head as it turns in keeping the eye on the approaching ball. The true pivot is actually a point in the region of the centre of the chest.

The Stroke. Before placing the ball for hitting, look at Plate XVIId and compare it with Plate XIc. You will see that the point of your shoulder comes half-your-shoulder's width in front of the contact-position in the similar off-side shot.

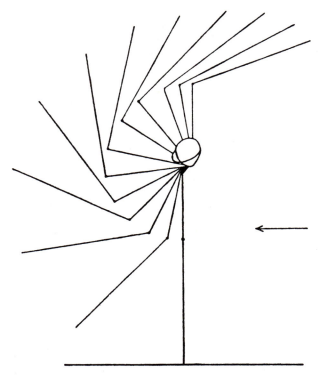

FIG. 11. NEAR-SIDE BACKHAND SWING

LOFT AND LENGTH

Your attention was drawn on pages 39 and 45 to an alternative method of placing the ball for stationary drives in the pit: namely, to place it six inches in front for forehand shots, or behind, for backhanders.

Figure 12 illustrates the effect of taking the ball at various distances in front of, or behind, the vertical contact-position.

The figure is an enlargement based on part of Figure 8, and shows the stick and the path of the stick-head near the vertical in a well-made drive,

STRIKING

in which the stick-head just grazes the ground at the vertical contact-position and completes the correct follow-through.

(a) and (d) show the stick and stick-head when the ball is taken fifteen inches on either side of the vertical contact-position.

The point of impact (being the point at which the line joining the centre of the stick-head[1] to the centre of the ball cuts the surface of the ball), is in both cases above the equator of the ball. In both cases, also, the line

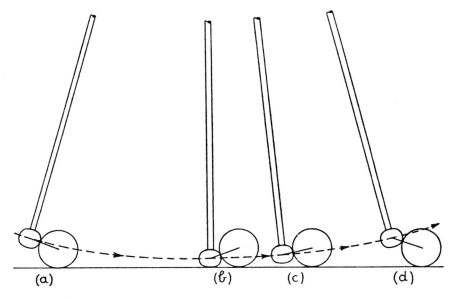

FIG. 12. POSITION OF BALL FOR LOFT AND FOR LENGTH

joining the centres is sloping steeply downwards by the same amount, showing that to hit the ball above its equator tends to drive it into the ground.

You will notice that in (a) the stick is still on the downward path, whereas in (d) it is on the upward. In (a), consequently, the tendency to drive the ball into the ground is aggravated; and in (d) a considerable 'top spin' is imparted to the ball, which will tend to prevent it from rising.

In both cases, therefore, of taking the ball fifteen inches away from the vertical contact-position, the result will be to make it roll along the ground; and, owing to ground-friction, this will take away from the length of the

[1] The centre of the stick-head is only the mid-point in the case of a head of circular cross-section. An ellipse, having two foci, in the case of the R.N.P.A. head the expression centre of the stick-head must be taken as referring to the focus nearest the ball, as indicated in Fig. 12.

STRIKING

drive. If the ball is hit hard enough, as a matter of fact, it may bounce off the ground, but the top-spin on it will prevent it from travelling far.

Although length will be lost in both cases, this will be especially so in strokes that conform to (a): that is to say, in forehanders taken too far back, and backhanders taken too far forward.

(b) shows the stick and stick-head when the ball is taken in the vertical contact-position.

Here the point of impact is below the equator of the ball; and the line joining the centre of the stick-head to the centre of the ball is sloping steeply upwards, showing that to hit the ball *below* its equator tends to lift it into the air.

The movement of the stick-head is horizontal, and the application of this force below the equator imparts a considerable 'back-spin' to the ball, which aggravates its tendency to rise in the air.[1]

The lower the point of impact, also, the greater is the tendency of the ball to rise. In the vertical contact-position you have been taking the ball as low as you possibly could; for, since your stick has been grazing the ground anyhow, you could not have taken the ball lower without hitting the ground and arresting the motion of the stick. It follows, therefore, that in taking the ball in the vertical contact-position you have been giving it the maximum possible loft.

You were told to learn the strokes by taking the ball in this position, because it allows for the maximum of error. For if you take the ball too low, and hit the ground, your stroke is ruined anyway; whereas, if you take the ball too high, it is in the vertical position that you will have the greatest latitude of error before you 'top' the ball.

(c) shows the stick and stick-head when the ball is taken six inches beyond the vertical contact-position.

Here the point of impact is slightly below the equator of the ball, and the line joining the centre of the stick-head to the centre of the ball is sloping slightly upwards, showing that there is a definite tendency to loft the ball.

You will notice, however, that in this case the line of travel of the stick-head and the line joining the centres approximately coincide. The result of this is that practically all the force applied goes to make the ball travel, with a reasonable loft, little or none being expended in applying spin.

To sum up, then, the results of taking strokes in these various positions:

[1] The results of hitting the ball, on, above, or below its equator can be confirmed by applying the Theory of the Parallelogram of Forces.

STRIKING

Taking the ball too far beyond or before the vertical results in poor length and no loft;

Taking the ball at the vertical results in maximum loft, obviously at the expense of length;

Taking the ball beyond the vertical, at the point where the stick has started to travel upwards, but is still sufficiently near the ground to strike the ball below its equator, results in the maximum length compatible with a reasonable loft: enough loft, that is to say, to send the ball over the opponents' heads and make it difficult to meet.

This last position works out, in practice, to about six inches beyond the vertical contact-position: nearer the pony's head for forehanders, and nearer his tail for backhanders. This is the position recommended.

THE EFFECT OF A ROLLING BALL

You may have noticed that you can loft a rolling ball much more easily when you are reversing its direction, than when you hit it in the direction it is already rolling in. This fact is due to the spin on the ball.

A ball rolling along the ground must, of course, have top-spin on; and the vestige of this spin that will remain on the ball after you have struck it can either add to the loft on your shot, or diminish it.

If, for instance, you are overtaking a ball and hit a forehander, you will be hitting the ball in the direction in which it is already travelling; and the top-spin that remains will tend to keep the ball from rising. The same is true of a backhander at a ball you are riding to meet.

If, on the other hand, you take a forehand drive at a ball that is rolling towards you, you will be reversing the direction of the ball. The original spin on the ball will remain; but, considered in relation to the new direction the ball is travelling in, this will actually have become back-spin, which will tend to loft the ball. The same is true of a backhand shot at a ball which is travelling in the direction you are riding.

Another consideration in this connection is the tendency of the ball to roll slightly up onto the top of the stick-head when the direction is being reversed, which allows the head to get further underneath, thereby increasing the loft. Conversely, if the ball is rolling the other way, there is a tendency for the stick-head to climb above the equator of the ball, keeping the ball down.

STRIKING

CUT AND PULLED STROKES

Cut shots are taken well out from the pony's side: to the rear for forehanders, and to the front for backhanders.

Pulled shots are taken close in to the pony's side: to the front for forehanders, and to the rear for backhanders.

In making the four drives, you should have had little difficulty in keeping the stick-head in the correct plane; but when you are taking cut and pulled shots you will find further consideration necessary.

In cutting, for instance, you may have difficulty in getting the early part of the stroke in the correct plane, since your stick is apt to foul the pony's body. This difficulty is illustrated in Plate XXIe, which illustrates an off-side forehand cut-shot about to be made, with the ball being taken far out and back. The greater the cut you want to make, therefore, the further out from the pony's side you must take the ball; and in an extreme case you may even have to twist the stick slightly in your hand, so as to give the ball a glancing blow. This will increase the angle of the cut, though at the expense of length and, to some extent, of accuracy. Plate XXIf illustrates a near-side backhand cut shot about to be made.

In pulling, the early part of the stroke should present no difficulty, but your follow-through may be interfered with by your pony's body. You should, therefore, take the shot well in to his side: forward in a forehander, so that the stick can follow through clear of his front legs; and well back in a backhander, so that it can follow through clear of his hindlegs. In extreme cases you will find it necessary to swing the pony's quarters away from the backhander.

THE DIAMOND RULE

If you look at Figure 13 on p. 54, you will see that the cut and pulled shots, which have to be taken at points sloping gradually outwards from in front and behind you, fit, when taken in conjunction with the four drives, into a diamond-pattern.

Figures 13a, 13b, 13d and 13e show the positions for the four fundamental strokes, each with its three subdivisions; and the central Figure 13c, shows the twelve principal strokes in the game, united.

You cannot do better, when practising pulled and cut shots, than place the ball in accordance with Figure 13c; and if you think of these shots as

STRIKING

a

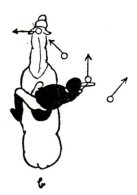
b

c

d

e

FIG. 13. THE DIAMOND RULE

STRIKING

lying along an imaginary diamond drawn on the ground around you, it will help you when you come to taking cut and pulled shots in the game.

Notice that the diamond is not a regular one; the left side is in advance of the right, owing to the shoulders being turned parallel to the pony in the near-side shots. When placing the ball for these shots, also, you may find that the distance between the positions for your forehand and backhand drives exceeds the twelve inches you would expect from taking the ball six inches beyond the vertical contact-position. If this is so, it will be because the point of your shoulder is being brought slightly further back at the contact-position in backhanders, as explained in the section on the Brace.

The figure shows that in extreme cases, when you want to pull the ball at a right-angle or more with a forehander, you must place the ball as far forward as possible, and towards the centre line of the pony.

These shots are known as 'under-the-neck' strokes.

THE OFF-SIDE UNDER-THE-NECK STROKE

The off-side under-the-neck stroke is illustrated in Plate XIII.

This shot is made along much the same lines as the off-side forehand drive.

Starting at the usual preparatory position, as in Plate XIIIa, lean forward at the top of your swing (Plate XIIIb). The plane of the swing will be turned through a right-angle.

Rotate your body about your head, as usual, bringing the right shoulder well down over the pony's neck (Plate XIIIc).

The contact-position should be well forward, and actually on the centre line of the pony, as in Plate XIIId. Keep your hand *well down*, so that you can make a good follow-through, as in Plate XIIIf.

THE NEAR-SIDE UNDER-THE-NECK STROKE

The near-side under-the-neck stroke is illustrated in Plates XIX and XX.

Start the stroke by pointing the stick forward (see Plate XIXa), in much the same way as at the top of your swing in the ordinary near-side forehand drive. An alternative way of starting the stroke is shown in Plate XXa, in which the head of the stick is kept up.

At the beginning of the stroke the body must be leaned well forward,

STRIKING

and the right shoulder brought well over to the left (Plates XIXb and XXb).

At the contact-position, the ball should be well forward; but this time slightly to the left of the pony's neck (see Plates XIXd and XXd, and Figures 13a and 13c).

The stroke is made like an ordinary near-side forehander, with the plane of the swing, however, turned through a right-angle; and the follow-through (Plates XIXf and XXf) is as important as ever.

'FANCY' STROKES

There are a few fancy strokes in the game, of which the following may be useful for you to know:

(a) *Away-from-the-neck Shot.* In order to avoid having to tap the ball with a difficult cut-shot when you want to turn and keep possession of the ball, an 'away-from-the-neck' shot can be made.

Get into the contact-position for an under-the-neck stroke, and swing the stick across under the pony's neck. This will bring you into a position resembling that shown in Plates XIIIe and XXe. Then swing the stick back again, making a half-shot.

In this way, you can take a shot at a right-angle, or more, to your line of travel, when the ball is too far over on the side you want to hit to, for an under-the-neck shot to be possible.

As by Field Rule 19 (pages 129 and 160) your opponent may not hook your stick unless he is on the same side of you as the ball, this stroke has the merit of securing immunity from having your stick hooked.

(b) *Push Shot.* When you are being ridden on the near quarter, you will sometimes want to tap the ball diagonally across your line of advance, over to the off-side, by means of a half-shot.

To avoid interference, you will have to take this shot well up along the pony's neck. It is a sort of 'push shot', and is made from the right elbow, which should be held well forward.

On the off-side a rather similar shot can be taken, but in this case entirely with the wrist.

(c) *Jab Shot.* When two opponents are racing for possession of the ball they will, as a rule, mutually interfere with the other's shot, unless one player can extend his reach beyond the other's. To do this some players employ a 'jab shot', that is, they lean as far forward as they can (at least as far forward as in Plate XIIId) and extend the arm and stick in one straight line at the

STRIKING

ball, making a jab at it, rather in the manner of a tent-pegger. This shot gives the player the longest possible reach and, unless it is quickly countered, will enable him to send the ball clear of his opponent.

(*d*) *Disengage Shot.* When an opponent is obviously preparing to hook a player's stick, the latter may be able to defeat him by making an early 'feint' at the ball, in order to draw his opponent's stick early, somewhat as in fencing. The Player then disengages and beats off his opponent's stick hard, in time to leave the way clear for a quick half-shot.

(*e*) *Between-the-legs Shot.* You may sometimes want to take a shot under the pony's belly.

Take care, if you do this, that the ball does not hit one of his legs. And do not follow-through, in case you should trip the pony with your stick: this is the *one* case in which neglect of your follow-through is permissible.

You may be able to play the shot so that the stick 'fetches up' against your foot immediately after impact with the ball, and in that way stop the follow-through, but a safer way is to play so as to hit the ground deliberately at the same moment as the ball.

On either side of the pony the *normal* grip must be used.

QUICKNESS IN STRIKING

It must be realised that the explanations given of the fundamental strokes apply to the full drive under ideal conditions, when you are not being interfered with and have plenty of time. Needless to say, it frequently happens in the course of play that, owing to threatened interference, any sort of quick stroke is of greater importance than a perfectly made swing which is hooked or ridden off. In such a case you are recommended to dispense with the full swing and follow-through, in order to make any quick stroke (even if it be only a wrist-shot) that will serve. Openings, in fact, frequently come so unexpectedly that there can be no question of fully turning the body and starting from the top of the swing, and the situation has to be dealt with by short, quick half-shots or possibly by dribbling the ball. Avoid dribbling as much as possible; it is far more difficult in polo than in hockey or football, but may at times be of value, if you have become good at it.

THE STROKES ILLUSTRATED

The following photographs are taken from a slow-motion film of the strokes, made by Lord Wodehouse (dark vest) and Mr. Winston Guest (in white).

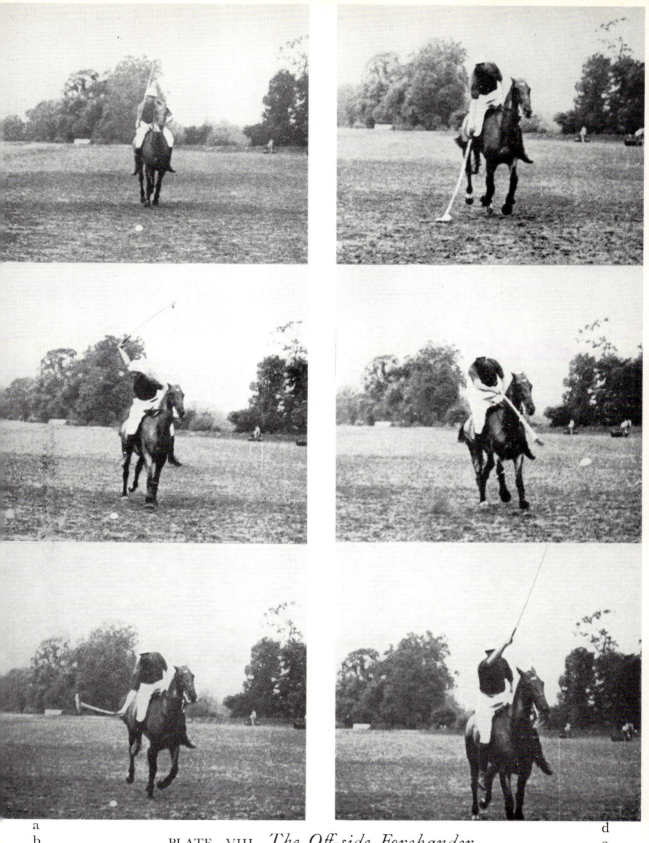

PLATE VIII *The Off-side Forehander*

a
b
c
PLATE IX *The Off-side Forehander*
d
e
f

a
b
c
PLATE X *The Off-side Forehander*
d
e
f

a b c PLATE XI *The Off-side Backhander* d e f

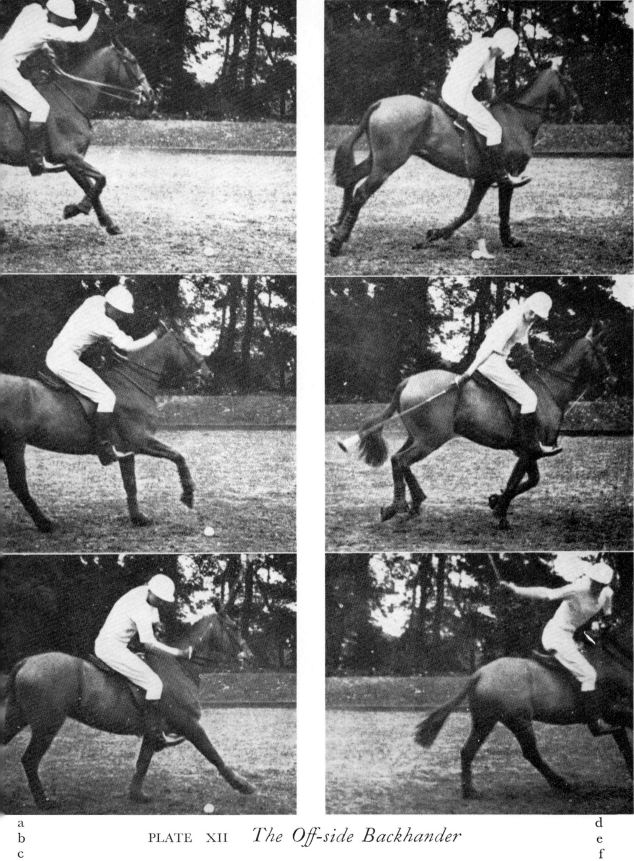

a
b
c
PLATE XII *The Off-side Backhander*
d
e
f

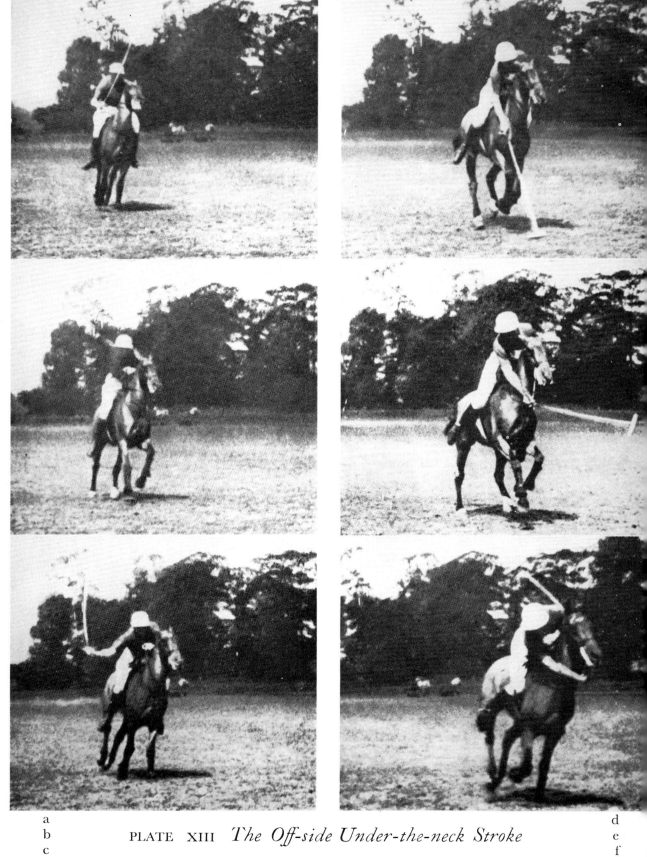

a
b
c
PLATE XIII *The Off-side Under-the-neck Stroke*
d
e
f

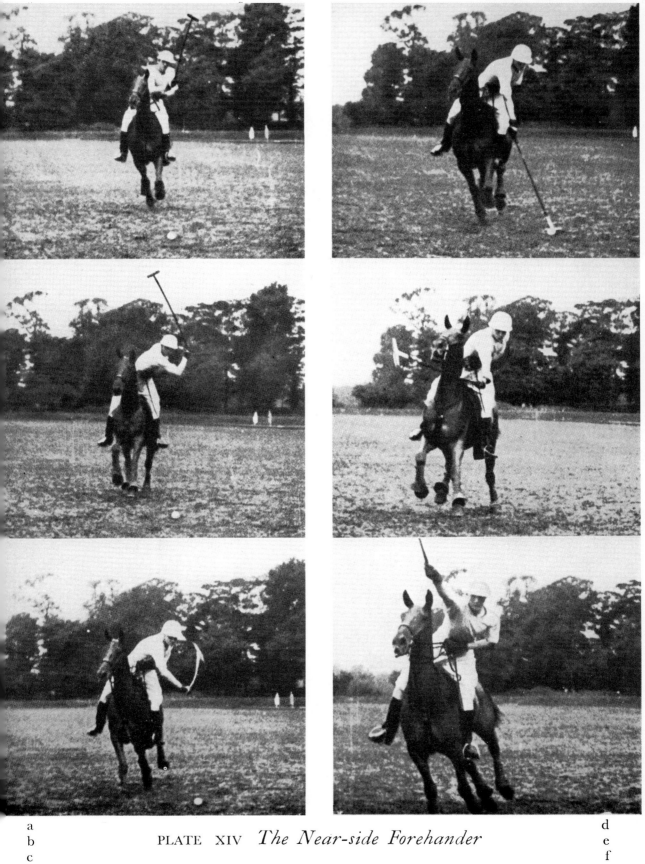

PLATE XIV *The Near-side Forehander*

a
b
c
PLATE XV *The Near-side Forehander*
d
e
f

a
b
c
PLATE XVI *The Near-side Forehander*
d
e
f

PLATE XVII *The Near-side Backhander*

a b c   d e f

a
b
c
PLATE XVIII *The Near-side Backhander*
d
e
f

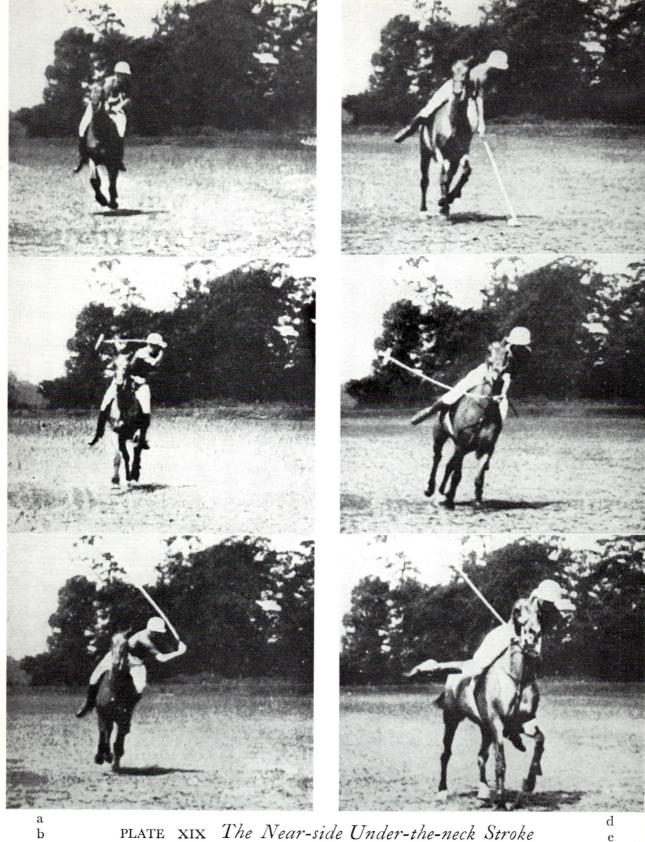

PLATE XIX *The Near-side Under-the-neck Stroke*

a
b
c

d
e
f

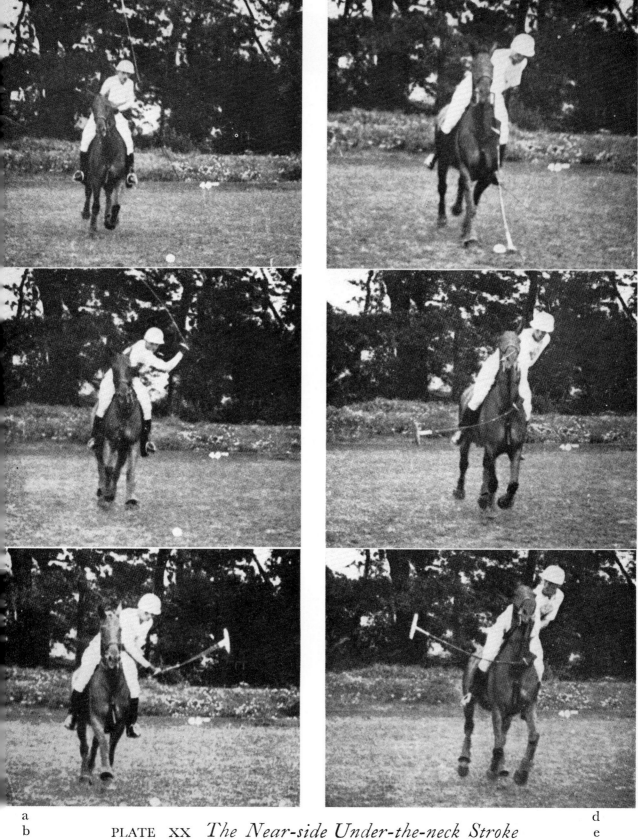

a
b
c
PLATE XX *The Near-side Under-the-neck Stroke*
d
e
f

a
b
c
PLATE XXI *Supplementary Views*
d
e
f

PART TWO

CHAPTER FOUR

THE GAME

BEFORE you start to play, watch a few games, preferably in the company of someone that can explain the game to you as it develops. The higher the standard of play you watch, the more easily you will understand what is happening; and one match between good teams will give you a better object-lesson than a number of indifferently played 'club chukkas', or 'members' games'.

When you watch good polo, do so from a good vantage-point, such as the top of a stand, or from a bank, so that you may get as complete a picture as possible of what is happening simultaneously all over the ground. If you accustom yourself to watching the game from a 'bird's eye' point of view, you will be developing a faculty you will find extremely useful when you come to play.

If you have never seen polo played before, and can find no one that will trouble to explain the game to you point by point, the explanation that follows should enable you to watch with advantage, and should be a help to you when you start playing.

The full Rules of Polo issued by the Hurlingham Polo Association are given in Appendix III; and then the rules issued by the United States Polo Association are given in Appendix VI; but this chapter explains all the rules with which, as a beginner, you need concern yourself.

The lay-out of the ground is shown in Figure 14, on page 65. There is a safety zone, which extends beyond the field of play to a distance of about ten yards from the boards or side lines and about 30 yards from each goal line. No one is allowed within the safety zone during play except the players, umpires, referee, goal judges, manager and stickholders; and of course no one is allowed on the ground itself except the players and umpires.

THE TEAM

Each team consists of four players, numbered from 1 to 4.

Numbers 1 and 2 are the forwards, Number 3 the half-back, and

THE GAME

Number 4 the back (the latter being more usually referred to as 'Back' than by his number).

THE UMPIRES AND REFEREE

In less important matches there may be one umpire, who is mounted and on the field of play, and whose decision is final.

In more important tournament matches, however, there are two umpires; and a referee is also appointed, who watches the game from off the field of play, and whose decision, in the event of the umpires' disagreeing, is final.

THE DURATION OF PLAY

The game is divided officially into 'periods' often colloquially referred to by the Indian name 'chukkas'. General Rule 7 (a) lays down that the duration of actual play is 42 minutes divided into 6 periods of 7 minutes each. The U.S.P.A. Rules specify 3 minute intervals and 5 minutes at half-time. When the timing clock is stopped, on the umpire blowing his whistle, this time is not counted in the playing time. The clock is re-started when the ball is put back into play, thus the chukka is prolonged by this amount. At the end of 7 minutes a bell is rung or a horn sounded while play continues, until the ball goes out of play. If it has gone out of play within 30 seconds a second bell is sounded and the chukka stops at the first stroke. Local committees often reduce the number of chukkas in a match.

These divisions of the game are necessary, since a pony galloping and turning at full speed, with the weight of a human on its back, cannot safely play for longer without resting. A pony is not played in more than two chukkas on the same day, unless there are exceptional circumstances, and it should be given as long a rest as possible between periods of play.

At the end of seven minutes a horn is sounded (U.S. Rules) or a bell may be rung (Hurlingham Rules).

Play continues until the ball goes out of play or strikes the boards, but if still in play after thirty seconds a bell is rung and play stops on the first stroke. However, in the last period of a match play ceases the moment the horn or first bell is heard, except in the case of a tie, when play continues as usual, and, if the game is still undecided, one or more further periods are played, the game finishing when the winning goal is scored.

In club-chukkas or members' pick-up games, play usually finishes in each chukka as soon as the bell is rung or the horn is sounded.

THE GAME

SCORING

A goal is scored when a ball passes between the goal posts and over and clear of the goal line. If a ball is hit above the top of the goal posts, but in the opinion of the Umpire between those posts *produced*, it counts as a goal.

The side that scores most goals wins the game, of course.

HANDICAPPING

Each player is given a handicap of 'minus 2 goals', through 'minus 1 goal' and 'nought' to '10 goals'. Handicaps issued by the Hurlingham or U.S. Polo Association are recognised internationally, but some clubs issue, for local use in their own clubs local handicaps which are higher than the above (e.g. the Author in 1938 had a handicap of 5 in the Hurlingham list, 8 in Malta and 9 in Jamaica).

When the third edition of this book was being written the last full handicaps lists published in all parts of the world in 1939 included some seven thousand players. There were only nine players with a handicap of 9 or 10 and only ninety of 6, 7 or 8. Ninety-two players were handicapped at 5 and all the remaining six thousand eight hundred odd were handicapped at 4 goals or less.

In matches played on handicap, the individual handicaps in each team are added together, and the smaller total is subtracted from the larger; the stronger team then concedes the weaker a 'start' of the difference in goals. Since all handicaps are based on the assumption that a full match will be played, this start must be proportionately reduced when fewer chukkas are played. All fractions of goals thus obtained are reckoned as half-goals in Hurlingham general Rule 7(b) but in U.S.P.A. general Rule 7b it states that fractions of a goal of a half or more shall be counted as a goal. By implication fractions of less than half-a-goal are not counted at all.

INDOOR POLO

In Indoor Polo, which is extensively played in the United States and Argentina, the team consists of three players. The system of handicapping is the same; but the handicaps in one are not necessarily applicable in the other (viz. Mr. Winston Guest, who was in the year 1930 the only player in the

THE GAME

world handicapped officially at 10 in Indoor Polo, was then a 9 at Outdoors Polo).

The game is played with the usual polo-sticks, but with a larger ball ($4\frac{1}{2}$ inches in diameter) made of sponge rubber covered with leather.

The goal-posts are 10 feet apart, and the standard arena is only 300 feet by 150.

The official manual of the Indoor Polo Association of the United States, prints in full the rules of the game.

THE THROW-IN

The game is opened by the umpire, who bowls in the ball underhand between the opposing teams.

The teams are lined up, facing one another, in the centre of the ground, each player being paired-off opposite his corresponding number. The conventional order for the line-up is 1, 2 and 3, in that order; the Backs keeping more towards their own goals (as in Figures 17 to 20, on pages 90 to 93).

THE GAME OPENS OUT

Once the ball is struck, and the game opens out, the players no longer mark their corresponding numbers, as at the line-up, but their opposite numbers: Number 1 marks the opposing Back, 2 the opposing 3, and so on, as shown in Figure 14.

You will see that as the ball is passed up from one player to another, the forwards disengage from their opposite numbers and gallop up clear for a pass, when they are in attack; but that as soon as their attack is stopped they immediately cover their opposite numbers again, in defence. When the ball is finally passed into the centre by the attackers, there must always be at least one player (usually Number 1), lying ready to receive the pass and shoot at goal. You will notice that the defenders try to clear their goal by hitting the ball out to the sides.

The players normally keep well spaced-out, and in their correct order, each Number 1 being nearest to the enemy goal, and each Back nearest his own. In well-organised teams, adjacent players on the same side will frequently exchange positions for a few moments, when the tactical situation makes this necessary; but you need not worry about this aspect of the game until you have played a certain amount, and have picked up some of the principles of team-play.

THE GAME

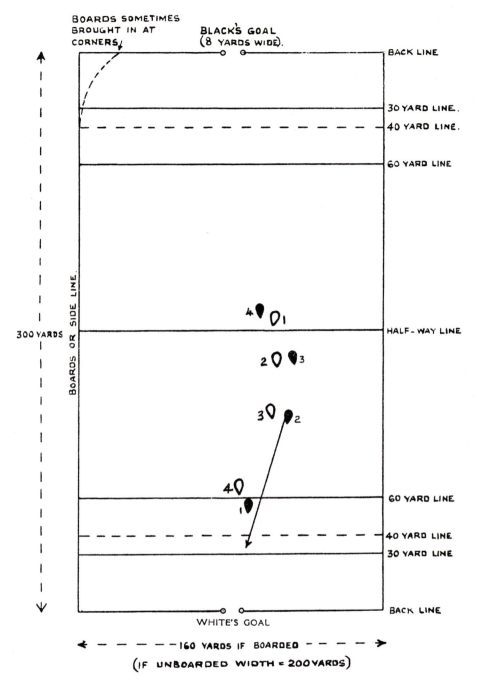

FIG. 14. THE GAME OPENS OUT

THE GAME

When you have managed to get a comprehensive view of the game, try to look at it as if you were taking part: put yourself in the place of various players, and try to see their actions from their own point of view. Watch Number 1 particularly closely. Whichever position you aspire to play in eventually, you are sure to serve your apprenticeship at 1, as it is the easiest place to start playing in. Notice that 1 sticks closely to the enemy Back, slipping him and galloping up for a pass when his side is attacking, and turning quickly, riding back, and closely marking the Back again when his side is forced into defence.

BALL OUT OF PLAY

When the ball is struck over the boards (or over the side line, if the ground is not boarded), the two teams line up again, as at the beginning, five yards from the boards and opposite the point at which the ball went out of play. The ball is then thrown in between the players, and the game continues.

When a chukka ends with the ball still in play, the game is reopened with the players lined up as at the beginning; but in such a case the ball is thrown in, towards the nearest side, from where it lay when the whistle was blown for play to stop.

When a goal is scored, the teams change ends and line up again as at the beginning. (This frequent change of end is often confusing to the beginner.)

In club-chukkas, if no umpire is present, the team that has just scored usually hits the ball in from behind its new back line, to save time.

When neither side scores a goal, ends are changed at half-time (see Hurlingham Field Rule 9[1]); though some clubs have a local rule that ends shall be changed only after each chukka, and not at half-time, on days when there is a strong wind blowing up and down the ground.

If the ball is hit behind the back line by the attacking side, the defending side hits in from the point at which the ball crossed the line, but in no case nearer than four yards to the goal-posts or the boards.

CROSSING

When players, each bent on being the first to reach the ball, are riding at it from different directions, the chances of collision are very great;

---

[1]U.S.P.A. Field Rule 8(a) states that the team which has lost the toss at the beginning of the game may elect, when the game continues after half-time, which goal to defend.

THE GAME

definite 'Rules of the Road' have therefore been established and are explained very fully in Field Rule 16. This is one of the most important rules in Polo and used to be so difficult to follow that the International Rules Committee redrafted it entirely. This rule, which is given on page 127 should in due course be carefully studied in conjunction with the diagrams given on pages 133 to 139. American readers should study pages 159 and 165 to 169. An abbreviated explanation of the rule is given below.

At each moment of the game a 'Right of Way' exists, extending ahead of the player entitled to it and in the direction in which he is riding. This Right of Way is not to be confused with the line on which the ball is travelling, and does not necessarily depend on who last hit it. No player may enter, or cross, this Right of Way, except at such a distance that not the slightest risk of collision, or of interference with the stroke of the player entitled to the Right of Way, is involved.

Possession of the Right of Way entitles a player to take the ball on the off-side of his pony. If he rides to take it on his near-side, and thereby in any way endangers another player, who would otherwise have been clear to take it on his off-side, he automatically loses his Right of Way, and must keep clear of the other player.

The player *following* the ball on its exact line, and taking it on his off-side, is entitled to the Right of Way over all other players. A player riding to *meet* the ball on its exact line, and taking it on his off-side, will be clear of the player entitled to the Right of Way, and is therefore entitled to share it with him. The only exception to this is when the player following the ball on its exact line has another player with him, trying to ride him off; in this case these two must be given way to by all other players.

Players riding from opposite directions on the exact line of the ball must 'keep to the left', and each must take the ball on his off-side, so that they shall be clear of one another.

If no player is riding exactly on the line of the ball, then the player *following* it at the smallest angle to its line is entitled to the Right of Way, which it should now be noted crosses the line on which the ball is travelling.

Where no player riding in the general direction in which the ball is travelling is near enough to risk a collision with players riding to meet the ball at an angle, the Right of Way passes to whoever of the latter is *meeting* it at the smallest angle.

If another player can enter the Right of Way safely ahead of the player entitled to it, he may do so; so long as he does not check his pony he then takes over the Right of Way and may not be ridden into from behind. No

THE GAME

player may check, or pull up on, or cross the Right of Way, if by so doing he runs the least risk of colliding with the player entitled to it.

When you hit backhanders you will find that your pony tends to swing over slightly to the side on which you are hitting; but you must not form the habit of turning in that direction. In the game, if there is a player closely following the original line of the ball, you will be committing a foul if you cross this line, even if you have just hit the ball in a new direction; and this can be a dangerous foul. Make a point, therefore, of turning *away* from the side on which you have just taken the ball: you will then be less likely to commit this foul.

DANGEROUS RIDING

Field Rule 17 forbids dangerous riding, such as:

(*a*) Bumping at an angle dangerous to a player or to his pony;

(*b*) Zigzagging in front of another player who is riding at a gallop in such a way as to cause the latter to check his pace or risk a fall;

(*c*) Pulling across or over a pony's forelegs in such a way as to risk tripping him;

(*d*) Riding an opponent across the Right of Way;

(*e*) Riding at an opponent in such a manner as to intimidate him and cause him to pull out, or miss his stroke, although no foul or cross actually occurs.

(*f*) Sandwiching, i.e. two players of the same team riding off an opponent at the same time.

It should be noted that U.S.P.A. Field Rule 17 does not include this (*e*) or (*f*) but has a different wording to their (*e*) 'Lack of consideration for safety on the part of a player for himself, his pony, or for other players and their ponies'.

ROUGH HANDLING OR PLAY

Field Rule 18 forbids rough handling, such as seizing with the hand, striking, or pushing with the head, hand, forearm or elbow. When riding-off another player, it is permissible to use the arm above the elbow; but the elbow itself must be kept close to the side.

MISUSE OF STICK

It is legitimate, and in fact 'good polo', to prevent another player from

THE GAME

hitting the ball by hooking his stick with your own; but this is only allowed if he is in the act of striking, and if you are on the same side of him as the ball (see Field Rule 19), or in a direct line behind him.

You must take care to keep your stick from getting across the legs of his pony, and see that it is neither over nor under the pony's body.

When riding a pulling pony, if you should have to put your stick-hand on the reins, don't let your stick lean out when you are riding-off an opponent, for if it becomes entangled with his, at the moment he wishes to make a stroke, this will constitute a foul against you.

You are not allowed to put your stick across any part of an opponent's pony to strike at the ball, nor may you hit into or amongst the legs of another player's pony. If, however, you have the Right of Way, any player who rides into your backhander does so at his own risk.

If your pony requires urging on, or possibly punishment, you must use a whip, for you are not allowed to strike it intentionally with your polo stick.

Field Rule 19 (d) forbids your using your stick dangerously. No example is quoted, but an obvious one is taking a full under-the-neck stroke when being ridden off, since the stick is likely to bend round and hit your opponent in the face. This danger is well illustrated in Plates XIIIf and XIXf.

APPEALING FOR FOULS

General Rule 5 not only confines to Captains the sole right to discuss any questions arising during the game with the Umpire but expressly forbids you to appeal for fouls in any manner (even by holding up your stick at arms length).

DISMOUNTED PLAYER

Lest a player should throw himself off his pony at a critical and disadvantageous moment to obtain a respite for his side (a thing which was formerly not unknown), the game is nowadays no longer stopped if a player falls off, unless the pony falls too, or unless the player is knocked off by another player or injures himself by his fall (see Field Rule 22).

No dismounted player may hit the ball or interfere in the game (see Field Rule 21).

THE GAME

PENALTIES

Breaches of Rules are, of course, penalised. The penalties are given numbers from 1 to 10, and the H.P.A. also give short names, e.g. 'Penalty 2: 30–yard Hit.' Basically, Penalties 1 to 6 are the same in both the H.P.A. and U.S.P.A. rules and these are given below in an abbreviated form.

The differences in the higher numbered rules and comparatively small differences in the lower numbered rules are very fully explained in Appendix VIII, 'H.P.A. and U.S.P.A. Penalties compared'.

But a beginner need not bother his head about the differences since the umpires will always indicate not only the Penalty Number awarded but will supervise its correct carrying out.

Penalty 1: Penalty Goal. The side fouled is given a goal.

Penalty 2: 30-yard Hit. A free hit, 30 yards from the centre of the fouler's goal, or from where the foul took place. The fouling side stay behind their back line and may not ride out through the goal. The side fouled keep to their side of the 30-yard line.

Penalty 3: 40-yard Hit. The same as Penalty 2, but 40 yards from goal, instead of 30. The usual position for players are shown in Figure 22 on page 95.

Penalty 4: 60-yard Hit (Opposite Goal). A free hit, 60 yards from the centre of goal. Foulers may not be within 30 yards from the ball; the side fouled anywhere.

Penalty 5: Free Hit: May be taken (a) *from spot* where foul occurred or (b) *from centre.* Foulers to be 30 yards from ball; side fouled anywhere.

Penalty 6: 60-yard Hit (Opposite where ball crossed). Given if one of the defending side hits the ball over his own back line, which in the U.S.A. is called 'hitting a safety'. In principle the same as Penalty 4, but ball is placed 60 yards from the back line opposite where it crossed.

The usual positions of players are shown in Figure 23, on page 96, which also gives a useful guide for Penalty 4.

THE FIRST GAME

Few polo-players, even first-class ones, will claim that they were not completely bewildered in their first game: so don't be depressed if you get thoroughly lost the first time you play.

THE GAME

Ultimately, you should aim at seeing the whole game in a mental picture, as if you were a spectator; but, as a beginner, you can hardly hope to keep track of seven other players simultaneously. You can at least try, however, to know where your opposite number is at any given moment, so that you can close with him quickly if your side is put on the defensive; and you should, in fact, have a guilty feeling whenever your opposite number has an unimpeded shot at the ball!

When you begin to play, as Number 1, stick closely to the opposing Back, and you will not go far wrong. In your first game, you should let yourself be guided to a large extent by his position, for he is likely to be an experienced player, who will keep in his place; and as he is the man you must mark, your place should generally be not far away.

There is no rule against riding a man, whether he has the ball or not. Don't forget this. You can make yourself extremely useful to your side, in your early games, even if you never hit the ball, by interfering constantly with the movements of your opposing Back. If he is handicapped at several goals more than you, and you succeed in neutralising him, you will in effect be scoring a corresponding number of goals for your side, in a handicap tournament.

Try always to know where the enemy goal is, so that you won't have to take your eye off the ball to look for it, just before you make a shot.

Your next step should be to include your fellow forward, Number 2, in your mental picture of the game; and so on, till you develop the faculty of forming a 'god's-eye' view of the game whenever you play.

CHAPTER FIVE

TEAM PLAY

As a beginner, playing in club chukkas and members' games, or in hastily improvised teams, you will have formed little idea of the pleasure and interest that are to be found in team play. But it is hardly too much to say that you will not really experience the charm of polo until you play the game as part of an intelligently organised combination.

Try, as soon as you can, to join a team that plays with agreed tactics, and in which the play of each member is helpfully studied and discussed; later on, perhaps, you may have occasion to form a team yourself, and pass on to others the fruits of your experience.

FORMING A TEAM

If the team is to function well, each member of it should be able to hit the ball on either side of the pony, and in any direction; though the pleasure of combined play can be experienced long before this stage of proficiency is reached.

The players should, if possible, be fairly evenly handicapped, since the team will be much better balanced and will play more satisfactorily, if one man does not have to 'carry the side'; and they should also be suited to play in the respective positions they will have to occupy.

The team should consist of friends, or of four people, at any rate, that are in touch with each other in their daily lives; for an organisation needs to be worked up in theory away from the ground as well as on it in practice. And for this reason it will be better to include a slightly less competent player, who is friendly and is prepared to exchange suggestions and advice, rather than a more competent one who resents criticism and is lacking in team-spirit.

Team-spirit is the first essential in a team player; and although it is a matter of character, it shows itself in so many ways that one can seldom be in doubt whether a player has it or not.

The selfish player, or 'ball-hunter', for instance, is easy to detect, and is best omitted from the side; so is the idler, who takes pains to make a

TEAM PLAY

sensational shot before the gallery, but not to ride his man when the ball is not near-by, and he thinks his movements are not conspicuous! Another kind of player best excluded is the persistent 'shouter'; for shouting in polo should be solely informative, and no one is so hard to play with as the man that is continually raising his voice.

The captain of the side, of course, should always be in a position to criticise; but even he should try and reduce his shouting to the minimum.

DISCIPLINE ON THE GROUND

The captain can better criticise the play of his team by holding a friendly post-mortem after the game, than by shouting at them and rattling them when their attention should be on what they are doing.

He should, of course, check a mistake that is being made, if there is time to prevent it; by telling a player to get back into his place, for instance, or to mark his man. But he should never criticise something that is done, and can't be undone, in the hearing of other people; except, possibly, in a practice-game, when he can ride over to the offender and point out the mistake in conversational tones.

On the polo-ground, the captain must be an absolute dictator. There can be no question of any discussion during the game; and he should expel the culprit, or resign, rather than allow a player to 'answer back'.

Consequently, it will be necessary that the team should have implicit confidence in his decisions. For this reason, it will be a good thing if he is the strongest player on the side; but he should, at any rate, be the most experienced. His experience will not depend so much on how long he has been playing polo, as on the intelligence he has brought to bear on the game, the amount of good polo he has watched, and the frequency with which he has exchanged opinions with other good players.

If the captain is to make his team feel that he really knows what he is doing, he will also need to have judgment, a capacity for leadership, and plenty of tact.

DISCIPLINE OFF THE GROUND

Away from the ground the discipline of the team will be on a different footing.

The captain will have to fill a double rôle. He will still be a dictator, but he must now be an arbitrator as well. He must encourage the team to air their grievances after the game, to ask his advice, and to consult him not only in matters that concern their play, strictly speaking, but in everything that could affect the success of the team in the field.

He should, for instance, make himself responsible, tactfully and without undue nursing, for the training and physical fitness of the players; and it is up to him to see that they arrive punctually on the ground.

He should call meetings after each match or practice-game, at which as many actual situations as the team can remember should be brought up and discussed. These can be reconstructed (with matches on a billiard-table, for instance), and in this way made more graphic and more intelligible. If in the game one player should wish to mark down for discussion something that is actually taking place, he can best fix it in the memory of the other players by saying, 'Remember that,' to them, as soon afterwards as he can manage.

At the meeting after the game it can be mutually decided whether or not the players, individually and collectively, acted in the wisest way; and, if not, how they might have done better. This should get each player used to the way in which each of the others tends to interpret the principles they have mutually agreed to follow; for it is only by discussing together the practical application of their theories, and by coming to know each other's idiosyncrasies, that they can make sure that in the game no action will be taken by one player, of which the motive is not immediately obvious to the others.

The captain must hold the balance of authority at these discussions, and decide, in cases where members of the team disagree, which of their opinions is to prevail.

THE BASIC PRINCIPLES OF TEAM PLAY

The following three axioms constitute the basic principles of team play, around which all theories of tactics have been built up:

1. *Always Place Your Stroke with a Definite Object.*

Hitting 'into the blue' is useless, or worse, since the ball may well go straight to where an opponent can get hold of it first.

There are only three possible objectives:

(*a*) To shoot at the enemy goal the moment you are within shooting-distance;

(*b*) To clear the ball to the side the moment it comes within shooting-distance of your own goal; and

TEAM PLAY

(c) To ensure that for every moment of the remaining time your own side shall retain possession of the ball.

Possession can only be retained if every shot is 'placed', either for a player on your own side, or, failing that, for your own second shot.

2. *Always Place Yourself with a Definite Object.*

If you are not in possession of the ball, there can be no question of your placing it; but you can very well place *yourself*, and this is, in fact, what you must do.

Riding into the blue is as useless and as mischievous as hitting wildly: and at every moment of the game you should be either where you deliberately intend to be, or else at full gallop on the way there.

It will depend largely on whether your side is attacking or defending, as to where and how you can place yourself with the greatest effect. In advanced attack, obviously, you will have to place yourself to the greatest advantage of your own side; whilst in desperate defence you will have to place yourself to the greatest *dis*advantage of your opponents.

But attack and defence are terms used to indicate the general direction the game is moving in: it does not follow, because you are in the enemy half of the ground, that you are in attack, nor are you defenders because you happen to be in your own half. As a matter of fact, attack and defence can alternate with almost every shot that is made; for the moment a long ball is hit and the players turn their ponies, attack has become defence, or vice-versa, no matter which half the game is being played in.

Consequently, it will often be hard for you to know, at a given moment, whether you should decide where to place yourself by considering your side in defence or in attack; and it will obviously be in most cases unwise to place yourself in such a way that, if the direction of play is suddenly changed, you will be unable to get back into your right place under the new conditions.

It is your instinctive solution of this constant problem, however, that will prove your value as a team-player.

3. *The Essence of Good Team Play is Flexibility*

If you are in attack, and find that no other player on your side is unmarked or in a good position to receive a pass from you, you may decide that you can only retain possession of the ball for your side by going through with it yourself. If you do decide to go on up with the ball, you will in effect be abandoning your position, and taking up someone else's; and your own position should immediately and automatically be filled by the player whose position you have taken over.

Similarly, if you are in defence, and are riding a man who goes through out of his position, you must keep on riding him, even if by doing so you are coming back out of your own. If you are brought so far back out of your position that you have virtually taken over someone else's, the player whose position you have taken over must realise that an exchange has been effected; and, the moment a back-hander is hit, and defence turns into attack, he must take up your old position and ride up forward instead of you.

A good rough rule for readjustment is that the player who has gone *forward* in the exchange should be the one to make the first move back into the original positions; unless, of course, the ball goes out of play, or else an obvious opportunity occurs for the player that dropped back to come through forward with the ball in the course of the game.

It is essential that the player whose position has been taken over, and the one that initiated the exchange, should both realise that they have exchanged full duties and responsibilities, and that they must discharge these conscientiously until the readjustment is made.

This system of free interchange is a very important factor in team play, and must be thoroughly understood and taken for granted by every member of the side.

A system of frequent and free interchange of positions is an important factor in team play; and this must be thoroughly understood and taken for granted, by every member of the side. It is much more important between the Number 3 and Back than between any other two players; and in their case this play may indeed be adopted as a team policy.

In the following chapters, whenever a player is referred to as 1, or as 3, you must understand that 'or *temporary* 1', 'or *temporary* 3' is implied; for whenever it is stated that he must perform certain duties, the reference will be to the duties of the position, and not of the player, who may not have started playing in that position, but may have assumed it or had it thrust upon him.

Flexibility in team play refers not only to the interchange of positions between players, moreover, but also to the transformation of the team as a whole. The team that can quickly reorganise itself in defence-formation, can afford to take greater risks in attack; and in the same way, it can take greater advantage of having stopped the enemy attack if it is quickly re-organised in attack-formation and makes immediate use of the turn in its fortunes.

TEAM PLAY

PASSING THE BALL

The first axiom of team play states that when you are not shooting at the enemy goal, or clearing your own, you must see that your side retains possession of the ball.

The first consideration arising from this statement must be when, how, and to whom to pass the ball when you let go of it yourself.

If you are going to pass, do so early. It is unlikely that you will remain for long in possession of it unmolested; so make your decision quickly.

Always pass the ball in such a way that the player picking it up can receive it easily: put yourself mentally in his place, and take the trouble to place it for him where you would yourself wish to have it placed for you. In most cases of passing the ball up forward, you should do so to the off-side of the player who is to pick up the pass, so as to give him the easiest shot, the off-side forehander; but if he is closely marked, you must, of course, send it to his disengaged side.

When you pass to a player quite near you, send a short pass wide of him rather than a long pass quite close to him, which an opponent may reach before he can overtake it. And when you pass to a player that is in a line with you more or less parallel to the goal-posts, pass well ahead of him: sufficiently ahead to give him time to take a full shot at it; and not so hard that it can overshoot him so far as to reach one of the defenders first.

In defence, never hit a backhander into the players that are following the ball. If you can look over your shoulder and see where your team are, pass to the disengaged side of your own forwards; if you can't look back, hit into the centre in the enemy half, and out to the boards in your own half. And if you can see the player who is to pick it up, always send a backhander sufficiently wide of him to give him room to turn on to the line of the ball.

A team that has played a great deal together can afford to adopt unorthodox tactics occasionally. For example, a backhander into the centre would normally be regarded as so risky in your own half, that your opponents would be disconcerted by it; but if your own team are expecting this play from time to time, and are ready to exploit it when it occurs, your opponents may be taken completely unawares and your side will get clean away in the unexpected direction. If such tactics are used too frequently, the element of surprise will diminish, and they will be less effective when they are really required: for instance, when the captain has ordered 'All Risks' to be taken (see page 87).

TEAM PLAY

WAITING, AND CALLING, FOR A PASS

When you are ahead of the player in possession of the ball, between him and the enemy goal, disengage yourself as soon as you possibly can, gallop up-field as far as you think he can hit to you, and wait for a pass.

The perfect pass will be a collaboration between the striker and yourself; for, just as you should pass in the way most convenient for the player picking up the shot, so, when you are waiting for a pass, you should try and place yourself where the striker can most easily hit to you, enabling him to concentrate as much as possible on the actual stroke.

If the player in possession seems in doubt as to where to pass the ball, and you are in a good position and unmarked, call to him for a pass.

Informative calling of this kind is particularly useful in the early stages of a team's practice; though when they have played together for some time, and begin to know each other's play, the need for calling should be less. It will always be useful, however, to call for a pass, provided that there is always sufficient justification for doing so. Your information will only be helpful if you are known to be reliable, and not given to calling for passes that you can't advantageously receive. When you do call, shout the player's name, *loud* (see page 105).

CENTERING

Figure 15, below, shows two players on a line parallel to the goal-posts, but of whom one is fairly central and the other out near the boards.

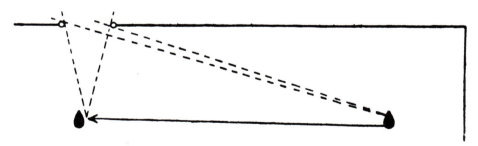

FIG. 15. THE ADVANTAGE OF CENTERING

You will see from the figure that the ball will be of little use to you in the enemy half if you are out near the boards; first of all, because you will be much further away from goal than your corresponding player in the centre, and secondly, because the goal will offer a much smaller target. Moreover,

TEAM PLAY

the angle subtended by the goal-posts will become smaller and smaller as you approach the back line; until, when you are quite near the back line, the angle will be so small that the goal will virtually be hardly 'open' at all. Remember this, and don't be tempted, when you see the goal-posts near you, into having a shot and hoping for the best, unless the goal is reasonably open to you.

Figure 16 shows that if a ball being centered either falls short of the centre-line, or overshoots it, the result will be less harmful if the pass has been made early; for the earlier, the more open the goal will be to the player picking up the pass.

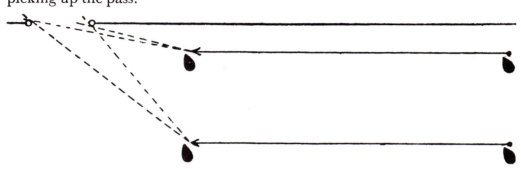

FIG. 16. THE REASON FOR CENTERING EARLY

Normally, if the player is in position to pick up the pass and you make it early enough, you should centre the ball with a forehander under your pony's neck.

But if a forehand pass would obviously be intercepted, or else if you have taken the ball so far up that there is a risk of its crossing the back line, you must centre it with a backhander under the pony's tail.

SHOOTING AT GOAL

The first axiom of team play states that you should shoot the moment you are within shooting-distance of the enemy goal.

This is indisputable; but you would do well at this stage to consider what the term shooting-distance actually implies. For it is not meant to define the *distance* of the ball from the goal, but rather the *combination of distance and direction* that is favourable to scoring a goal. Figures 15 and 16 illustrate the fact that you can be near the goal without being in a favourable position.

As a matter of fact, you can never make too certain of your shot; and if you have an *unhampered* shot at goal from 60 or 70 yards, there is no reason why you should not hit a 40-yard approach shot. This will leave you a tap-shot for scoring the goal, and will also provide you with a wider angle as a target; and it will also leave the ball in front of goal if you should miss your second shot, whereas if you had misdirected your first full shot, the ball would most likely have gone out of play.

No hard-and-fast rule can be laid down, of course: you will have to decide for yourself whether it is a good thing or not, in a given circumstance, to make an approach shot. But, whatever you do, don't throw away opportunities of scoring by being over-cautious.

When shooting at goal, don't forget that the forward movement of your pony imparts a movement to the ball in the direction in which you are galloping, and that this must be allowed for in any shot taken when you are not riding directly at the goal. The greater the angle between the centre of goal and the line you are riding on, the greater allowance you must make. The most usual case of this will be when you are riding parallel with the boards, and out of the centre: you must then aim at the further goal-post or, in extreme cases, even beyond it.

RIDING-OFF AND STICK-HOOKING

When you are marking a man, watch him carefully, and try and anticipate his movements.

Keep just in front of him, if possible, so that when you close with him your knee shall come just in front of his; and keep on his off-side for preference, so that he will have to take his shots on the near-side, whilst your off-side is left free.

You are allowed to close with him at any time; so you should do so before he shapes-up to take a shot or to receive a pass. Try and get in a good bump at a moment when he is least expecting it. This should disconcert him, and may make him divide his attention between the game and yourself at moments when it should be entirely on the game.

When you have slipped your man and ridden up in the attack, get back on to him quickly, the moment you are in defence again, and make up for lost time!

When hooking an opponent's stick, beat hard at it, instead of merely interposing your own. Remember not to break Field Rule 19, which lays down that this must be done on the same side of him as the ball. The best way to avoid having your own stick hooked is to use the 'Disengage Shot' described on page 57.

TEAM PLAY

COMBINED PRACTICE

The team should practise together: first, in pairs, the two forwards together, and the two backs; later, the pairs should interchange, so that each player may become accustomed to the style of the other three.

Each pair should practise picking up passes while riding fast, meeting backhanders, riding-off, and stick-hooking.

At first, when passing to a player behind you, you may need him to call for your pass, so that the sound of his voice may help you to gauge which direction to hit in. But you should practise looking back and estimating the direction before you take the shot; though you should not neglect the faculty of being able to judge direction by the voice alone, since you may have to pass to unexpected calls in the game, without looking back.

You may also find it difficult at first to place yourself for picking up a pass, without some indication being given by the other player, usually by pointing with his stick in the direction he intends to hit. But you must practise anticipating the strength of a pass and its direction by noticing the preliminary movements of the striker. It will be of the greatest value to you in the game that you should be able to turn in the right direction for a backhander, before the ball is hit.

The team should also practise together as a unit, placing themselves as for a hit-in, and taking the ball down the ground until a goal is hit. The player taking the hit-in should hit the ball to each of the other players in turn, to enable them to practise receiving it and hitting it on. This will also enable the remainder of the team to practise their appropriate moves. The player who receives the hit-in should pass the ball to 1, who should hit the goal; but if it is hit direct to 1, he should take it down the ground and hit the goal himself. (See also page 98.) Alternative plays will make it difficult for the opponents to foresee which particular play they will have to counter.

Combined practice is extremely important, especially when the side cannot get practice-games as a unit; for the most efficient team will deteriorate unless they have plenty of opportunity to play together.

ADVICE TO PLAYERS, INDIVIDUALLY

Number One. This is the easiest position in which to keep your place approximately (which is why you will probably play in it when you begin); but it is the hardest in which to keep your place accurately.

TEAM PLAY

You can be certain that you should always be the most advanced player on the side, and near the enemy Back; but you will find it hard to determine when to be ahead of him, level with him, or behind him.

This problem of how far to be an attacker, and how far a defender, is present in all four positions. But in yours it will be aggravated by the fact that, whereas you cannot be excused your fair share of defence, and will be expected not to let the enemy Back through, your principal function must be to score goals from passes, and to be lying up-field of the enemy, clear, when the pass comes.

Though you can only really solve this problem for yourself, with regard to the circumstances, the following may help you at first as a rough guide:

When your side is in attack, be ready to slip your Back. Keep a few yards to the side of him, and about half-a-length ahead. Don't gallop up-field at once, to wait for a pass that may never be made, and make it impossible for yourself to get back in time if your side's attack is stopped. But gallop up-field as far as you think a pass can reach you, the moment one of your side is in position to pass up the ball ahead of you and the enemy Back.

The nearer you are to the enemy goal, the further you can afford to be ahead of the opposing Back.

When your side is in defence, *close with your man*; but the moment you see that your Number 2 is going to be able to clear with a backhander, you must disengage. If it is your Number 3 or Back that is going to hit the backhander, you must be more cautious about turning up, as there will then be a greater risk of the enemy Back's meeting the ball successfully.

The nearer you are to your own goal, the more cautious you should be.

You will not be expected to perform the impossible feat of being right back in defence immediately after you have been waiting for a pass before the enemy goal-mouth, or vice-versa; but when your side is neither right up nor right back, you should try to keep your position as flexible as you can.

In placing yourself, you should assume that your side will hit a good long ball. You yourself need not be a particularly long hitter, but you must be able to shoot accurately at goal. To this end, you must practise shooting from every angle; and when practising with another player (preferably your own Number 2), you should learn to shoot from a pass as you pick it up.

Number Two. You will normally be the player to develop your side's attack: that is to say, when your side has been defending, it is usually to you that your 3 or Back will pass up the ball with a backhander.

For this reason you should be particularly quick in turning to a back-

TEAM PLAY

hander. Practise with your Number 3 and Back until you can tell from their preliminary motions whether they are going to cut or pull the backhander, so that you may turn accordingly.

If ever you allow the opposing Number 3 to get ahead of you when you are attacking, ride into his backhanders and keep trying to hustle him. If your 3 or Back can meet them successfully, it is not up to you to turn when your opposite number hits them, unless he himself turns.

In placing yourself, you should assume that your side will always succeed in hitting the ball, though you need not rely on their taking a more than average shot. You yourself will have to be a long and strong hitter, so as to be able to get the ball right up to your Number 1. Make use of him whenever you can, for if you try to hit all the goals yourself you will be making your team into a three-man side!

Number Three. You will be the pivot of the team: the link between the forwards and the Back. It will be your job to feed the forwards, to prevent an enemy attack from getting under away, and to turn defence into attack by a backhand pass up to your Number 2.

You will have ample opportunity to go through yourself in attack, and you must make the fullest use of it. You and the Back should practise going up to one another's backhanders, and interchanging freely, also making short passes across to each other.

You should turn to cover your Back when he is meeting the ball, for this will give him confidence when taking his shot and will reduce the risk if he should miss it. Always be prepared for your Back to miss a shot in defence, and ride to cover him until the ball is actually struck.

In placing yourself, you should assume that your side will make shots below the average, and that your opponents will make them above the average. You yourself must be a steady player, though not necessarily a brilliant one. Reliability in striking is more important for you than long hitting, and you must be the hardest worker on the side.

The Back. You can tackle your job in two ways: by staying well back, allowing your Number 3 to do all the half-back work, and only checking attacks that get past him; or else by playing half-back alternately with him.

Unless your Number 3 is a much stronger, more experienced, and better-mounted player than you, your captain is likely to direct you to follow the second plan, as it creates a far more difficult situation for your opponents to cope with.

In attack, you must always follow-up your side closely; for the Back

TEAM PLAY

often gets a shot at goal when the other players have all ridden each other over the ball!

Put in constant practice at meeting the ball. There is nothing that will turn defence into attack more effectively; but you should only do this if your Number 3 is turning to cover you.

In defence, you should be prepared for your 3 to miss his backhanders altogether, and continue to mark your opposing Number 1 until the ball is actually struck. You must then gallop up at full speed. When your Number 3 is taking his backhander in the enemy half, however, you will be justified in turning a little earlier, for the risk involved if he should miss the ball is not so great as in your own half.

You should be a long, reliable hitter, the accuracy of your shots being of minor importance.

GENERAL ADVICE

Always try, as you were told in Chapter 4, to have a mental picture of the game, or as much of it as you can manage to visualise. You should, at least, know at any given moment where your opposite number, your fellow-forward (or Back, as the case may be), and the enemy goal are. Otherwise it will be impossible for you to think one or two strokes ahead and take quick decisions; and in polo, half the battle is to decide quickly and to anticipate.

You will find it useful to have played, at one time or another, in every position, as this will enable you to appreciate its possibilities and recognise its difficulties.

When you are not the player that is actually going to pick up the ball, a good rough guide for turning, if you have no time to look over your shoulder, is as follows:

When your own side is hitting a backhander in defence, turn to the boards in your own half, and towards the centre in the enemy half. When the opponents are checking your attack with a backhander, turn to the boards in the enemy half, and to the centre in your own; but take care not to turn away from the man you should be marking.

If an opponent is about to take a backhander, when you are behind him in attack, turn at once if he is well ahead of you; but if he is fairly near, ride into the shot, so that your pony may stop it. This is rather hard on the pony, so you should only do this in match play: in a tournament, harden your heart, and ride your pony like a bicycle, without regard to considerations of this kind.

TEAM PLAY

There should never be more than two of your side in a scrimmage: of the remaining two, one must lie well up in the position of Number 1, waiting for a pass, and the other should keep back, in the position of Back, in case the opponents should get possession of the ball. If you are in a scrimmage and cannot hit the ball, beat at your opponents' sticks; but you should not undertake this until you are reasonably proficient in stick-hooking, and can be sure of not hitting your opponents' ponies.

When you are riding your man near the enemy goal, ride him clear of it: it is a hard enough target without ponies and riders as added obstructions. If you can't manage to get your opponent out of the way, the least you can do is to get out of the way yourself.

Conversely, when a shot is being taken at your own goal, you must try and ride your man into your goal-mouth, or block the space as much as possible by getting there yourself.

Sometimes a good player will feel that he can hit a short ball when he has no one to pass to, and does not want to hit far ahead to the opposing Back. But 'dribbling' the ball is a difficult art; and one, at all events, that should only be attempted on a perfect surface. If the ground is at all cut-up, hit the ball hard and gallop after it.

Remember, incidentally, that, unless you are taking an approach shot at goal or passing to a player who is across the ground from you (as explained in the section on Passing), you cannot hit too hard.

Don't slacken off for a moment in the game.

You may occasionally be able to keep your place and spare your pony in doing so; but there will never be a moment in which you cannot be doing something useful for your side.

It is never too late. Don't become resigned when your side is doing badly: and never stop playing until the ball is actually through the goalposts.

Whenever you are doing nothing, you are doing wrong!

DUTIES OF THE CAPTAIN

Nothing should be neglected that might contribute to the success of your team in the field.

Never feel that a piece of criticism or advice is too much trouble to give, or that it is too trivial, or that it exceeds your province.

Never feel that the interest you may show in a player, or the praise you may want to give, would not be appreciated.

TEAM PLAY

The *morale* of your team is of paramount importance.

First of all, insist on punctuality. See that the players are ready on the ground at least twenty minutes before a match. Nothing starts a team off so badly as the late arrival of one of the side. Conversely, nothing is better for a team than having time to get their eye in with a few shots, to try their ponies, and to get warmed-up and supple.

Arrange for stickholders to be placed at strategic points round the ground, with spare sticks for the whole team. If only one stick-holder is to be had, put him diagonally opposite to the ponies and the main dump of spare sticks.

See that each player moves quickly to his correct position for the hit-in and throw-in; the umpire will not wait for anyone that is slow in lining-up.

Use the pony-power of your team to the greatest advantage. After discussion with them, draw up a programme of training, and decide when team-practice shall start, and when the ponies should be brought up from grass at the beginning of the season, as a preliminary to playing in cantering games.

Before each important match, organise the order of play of each pony. This is extremely important, for between fairly level teams matches can be won or lost by the intelligent or haphazard order in which the available ponies are played. (See 'Considerations of Pony Power' on page 108.)

You can best captain the side if you play 3.

The side can be captained quite well from the Back-position, and fairly well from 2; but at 1 you will find control difficult, since you will never be able to see the side in attack.

As a matter of fact, you cannot expect to see all your team in attack and defence, whichever position you play in, since you can't be looking over your shoulder when you should be hitting the ball. If you feel that things are going wrong where you cannot see them, try playing a substitute in your position for a practice-game, and watching the game as an umpire, or from the side-boards.

Failing this, get some friend with a certain experience of polo to watch the team playing, and to describe to you afterwards the movements during the game of the players when you could not see them, especially in defence. You can then draw your own inferences, and see that the mistakes are corrected. (Some teams go so far as to have a team manager, or non-playing captain—usually a really experienced player, though possibly retired from active play. He fulfils all the functions of Captain off the ground; and may even dictate team policy between the chukkas of a match.)

TEAM PLAY

Make up your mind before a match which goal you will choose to defend if you win the toss. Wind and sun will be your chief variable factors: with little wind and the sun low, play with your back to the sun; and with a strong wind and the sun high, play as the wind suits you best.

Never tell your team that your opponents are giving you such a long start that you are sure to win if you only keep them out: if that is the spirit your team plays in, it stands a good chance of being beaten. As a matter of fact, 'attack is the best form of defence': and it will dishearten a team stronger than yourselves that you should score goals against them!

If the game starts going against you, don't let your team go to pieces. Take some definite action. A constructive change of policy (such as telling 1 to leave his man and go right up in attack, or 2 to go 'all out' for his man and keep him out of the game) will give them more encouragement than simply exhorting them to play-up when they probably feel they are already doing their best.

If you are slightly down, with not much time to go, it will be well worth while to risk another goal against you in a final desperate assault, and tell your side to take all risks. Since you may have to take this decision in play—for example if your opponents suddenly get a goal ahead, in the last chukka—it is as well to have a pre-arranged phrase such as 'All Risks', which you can pass quietly to your team.

However big your opponents' lead may be, never assume that you cannot catch up; and however far ahead your team may be, never think that your opponents cannot stage a come-back. You must not let your team give up hope when they are behind or relax when they are ahead: keep them playing full out until the final bell.

DRAWING-UP AN ORGANISATION

If a team is to function efficiently, it will have to follow some well-defined plan, or 'organisation'.

There are several recognised organisations: the 'column-game', developed by Cameron Forbes in Manila; the 'straight-to-goal' game, developed by Ricketts in Alwar; the Durham Light Infantry organisation, perhaps the most historic of all, developed by de Lisle; and others. . . .

The team may want, however, to amuse themselves by drawing-up their own organisation: its details are immaterial, so long as it embraces the general principles of team-play, and covers the following points:

TEAM PLAY

A scheme of attack;
a scheme of defence;
informative calling;
and considerations of pony-power.

A specimen organisation that has been tested and improved in the course of many years' play in different parts of the world, is outlined in the following chapter. It contains many of the generally accepted principles, and will serve as an example of the kind of organisation a team can draw up, as well as providing a rough guide for you if you are playing in a team that has not yet worked out a plan of its own.

As every eventuality in the game could not possibly be covered, however many instructions were laid down, it will be most satisfactory to build-up an organisation on as few detailed instructions as possible. But these must be based on sound principles, and must be understood and acted on by every member of the team.

Don't feel in reading the next chapter that you are going to find it difficult in the heat of the game to remember the tactics laid down in your side's organisation: there will (or should) be little in it that is not self-evident. Try to understand the commonsense principles on which it is built-up, and to assimilate the basic principles of team play that have been explained in this chapter. When you can put them into practice automatically, and leave your mind free for specified tactics, you ought not to find the latter more than you can cope with while a fast game is in progress.

CHAPTER SIX

SPECIMEN ORGANISATION

For the purpose of this specimen organisation, every situation has been considered from the point of view of attack, and from that of defence, *separately*; and these view-points have been embodied in the schemes of attack and defence respectively.

ATTACK

The primary factor in a successful attack is speed. The great thing is to waste no time in getting the ball to the enemy goal, and to give your opponents as little chance as possible to take up their defence-positions.

Generally speaking, if you are the stronger side you will be the attacking side, and it will be to your advantage to speed up the game. When you are the weaker side, however, you may sometimes feel that your advantage will lie in slowing up the game, and making it 'choppy'. But it will not do you much good to break up your opponents' attack, if you do not immediately counter-attack in your turn. In the following scheme of attack, therefore, it will be assumed that your team is intent on speeding up the play, whether in a given game they are the stronger team or not.

Your team must make up their mind that they will attack from the very moment the ball first comes into play.

To this end there must be a detailed organisation covering the eventualities of each of the four players being the one to meet the ball at the throw-in.

In the event, of course, of the ball being met by an opponent, your team will at once have to be organised in defence; and to this end, a detailed organisation must also be drawn up in your defence-scheme, covering the eventualities of each of the four enemy players being the one to meet the ball.

But the material advantage, to say nothing of the psychological one, of getting a good start, is enormous; and your team should determine at all costs to try and get away from the throw-in in attack formation.

SPECIMEN ORGANISATION

POSITIONS AT THE THROW-IN

Figures 17, 18, 19 and 20 show the attack-formations to be adopted at the throw-in.

Figure 17 shows Number 1 meeting the ball.

He must hit it out toward the boards at such an angle as to make sure that he can follow it up and take a second shot himself. Unless, therefore, he has managed to get his knee in front of his corresponding number's when they closed, and is able to get round him, he should not attempt to

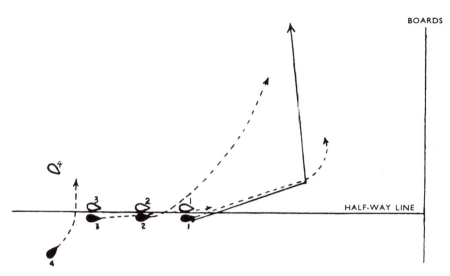

FIG. 17. NUMBER 1 MEETING THE BALL AT THE THROW-IN

hit the ball at more than an angle of 20 degrees to the centre-line, as shown in the figure.

When 1 follows the ball to take his second shot, 2 must force his way round in front of his corresponding number, and gallop up-field for a pass from 1; thereby exchanging positions with him.

Number 3 must back up the player in possession; and 4 must go up the centre.

When the ball has been hit out of play, and the Umpire is throwing it in from the boards, the same general scheme should be followed. It must be realised, however, that since the Number 1's will be only five yards from the boards, the first hit will bring the ball to the boards.

SPECIMEN ORGANISATION

Figure 18 *shows Number* 2 *meeting the ball.*

He must tap it towards the boards and follow it up for his second shot. The same considerations apply as for Number 1; and unless he can get round the man marking him, he should not hit the ball at an angle of more than 20 degrees to the centre-line, as shown in the figure.

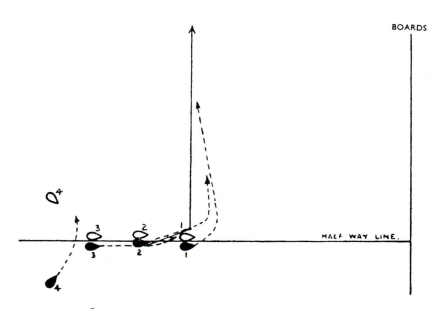

FIG. 18. NUMBER 2 MEETING THE BALL AT THE THROW-IN

(Though it may seem to you from the figure, that 2 would find it hard to get the ball before the opposing 1, this will not be the case, since all the players will be moving towards the boards.)

Number 1 must gallop up-field as far as he can expect a pass to reach him, for if he does not play a bold game he may be throwing away valuable openings.

Number 3 must again back the player in possession; and 4 must go up the centre.

If the Captain decides that he will want the ball to come through to the Back at the first throw-in, he should warn the team of this before they come on to the ground. Numbers 1, 2 and 3 will then have to ride their opponents off the line, to let the ball come through to the Back, who must move well up.

SPECIMEN ORGANISATION

Figure 19 shows Number 3 meeting the ball.

He also must hit it towards the boards, and the same considerations apply as for Numbers 1 and 2.

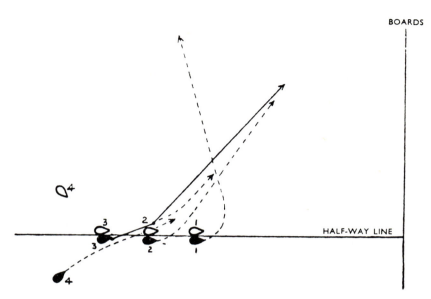

FIG. 19. NUMBER 3 MEETING THE BALL AT THE THROW-IN

Number 1 must gallop up-field and centre, and lie clear for a pass; while 2 also goes up, but more towards the boards, and 4 stays to back-up the player in possession.

Figure 20 shows Number 4 meeting the ball.

He will usually manage to do this only after a race to the ball with his corresponding Back; and in this case the way should be clear for him to hit towards enemy goal and take the ball through himself; or else, he may pass it to 1, if the latter is in a good position to receive it.

When 4 goes up in this way, 2 becomes 3, and 3 becomes the Back.

If the enemy Back, however, has gone back in defence instead of racing for the ball, 4 will have either to 'dribble' the ball to avoid giving the enemy Back a free backhander, or else he will have to hit wide for one shot and then pass it up to 1 when the latter has had time to get into position.

In no case, however, will 1, 2, or 3 take his first shot down the ground into the half where all four opponents are; unless Number 1 has made no

SPECIMEN ORGANISATION

attempt to meet the ball, but has broken forward at once into the enemy half and is waiting there for the pass.

When the ball is next out of play and is thrown in at the boards, the line-up will be the same as for the throw-in at the centre, and the team should again try at all costs to get away in attack-formation.

When the throw-in takes place within your own 30-yard line, however, the ball must on no account be allowed to come through into the centre. If it comes through to the Back he must hit it out to the boards again at once.

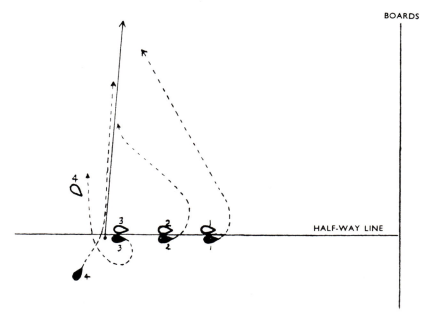

FIG. 20. THE BACK MEETING THE BALL AT THE THROW-IN

Whenever the throw-in takes place near the enemy goal-line, Numbers 1, 2 and 3 must push their opponents out of the way, to let the ball come through to the Back, if necessary passing it to him by means of a backhander. The Back must line up close to his Number 3, but facing the enemy goal, ready to get away and shoot at it.

NORMAL ATTACK-FORMATIONS

In the course of the game, the attack will usually tend to develop round Number 2, or 3 (generally the former), and on one of the flanks, or at any rate slightly out of the centre; since whichever side has been defending will usually have cleared the ball out towards the boards.

SPECIMEN ORGANISATION

Figure 21a *shows* 2 *in possession* when the attack develops.

Number 3 must back him up; and 1 must gallop on up-field and centre for a pass. (Compare with Figure 18.)

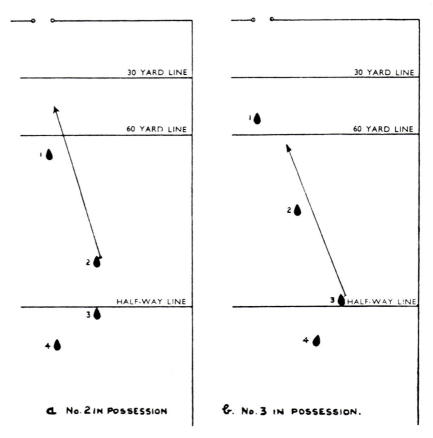

FIG. 21. NORMAL ATTACK-FORMATIONS

Figure 21b *shows* 3 *in possession* when the attack develops.

Number 1 must gallop as before; and 2 must ride on and place himself in as direct a line as possible between the ball and the enemy goal, as this is the line along which the ball should always travel if the speed of the game is to be maintained.

In both the above cases, you will notice, 4 keeps back and centre; but in the second case (compare with Figure 19), he must of course be ready to back-up 3 if the latter looks like being ridden off, or having his stroke interfered with before he can pass up the ball.

SPECIMEN ORGANISATION

The Back, in any case, should normally keep towards the centre, for he will then be on the shortest path between the two goals, and will be able to back-up the forwards in attack and get back quickly to his own goal if the attack is stopped.

When backing-up a player, don't keep too close behind him, but at a sufficient distance to enable you to take the ball and centre it if he should be ridden over it or have his stick hooked. You will see in the foregoing figures, that the players keep well spaced-out; at a distance of about 30 or 40 yards. You must take care, however, that no opponent manages to get between you and the player you are backing-up.

There should be an organisation dealing with the penalty and free hits and with the hit-in from your own back line. In the last two cases the team must be determined to get away in attack-formation.

POSITIONS AT THE 30-YARD, 40-YARD, 60-YARD, AND FREE HITS

Figure 22 shows the 40-yard hit; positions of the side fouled being shown in *black*. The positions for the *30-yard hit* are similar, except that the side fouled move forward ten yards. In neither case may any player cross the line until the ball has been hit or hit at. The two players nearest the goal-posts should try and stop the ball, but in riding out must not pass through the goal.

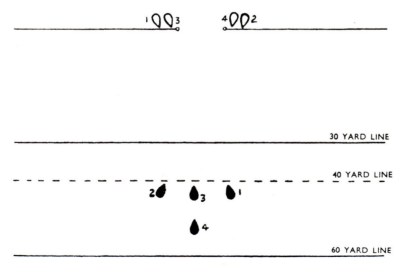

FIG. 22. THE 40-YARD HIT

SPECIMEN ORGANISATION

Figure 23 shows the 60-yard hit; positions of the side fouled being shown in *black*.

In all three cases the best striker on the side should take the shot although 3 has been shown as the striker in the figures. In the 60-yard hit, his two forwards should move to positions on either side of the goal, and face so that they can stop a misdirected hit from going behind.

The figure actually shows the 60-yard hit when it is for Penalty 6; but similar positions are taken up in Penalty 4, except that the ball, of course, will be opposite the centre of goal.

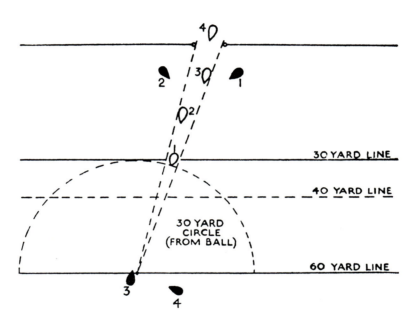

FIG. 23. THE 60-YARD HIT

Figure 24 shows the free hit from where the foul took place (Penalty 5). Only the suggested positions for the side fouled have been indicated. Either the Back or Number 3 can take the hit; but if the latter takes it, the Back must move up-field in the centre to the position marked 3.

The striker should hit to whichever player appears to be least effectively marked, or in the best position to slip his man. If there is a choice, the ball should not be hit to 1, for this will give him a chance to gallop well up-field to receive a pass from the player to whom the ball has been hit.

SPECIMEN ORGANISATION

The foulers may not come within 30 yards of the ball until it is hit. Their Back must stay well back; the other three should either mark the three opposing players waiting for a pass, or place themselves so that they can meet on its exact line a hit made to their nearest opposing player.

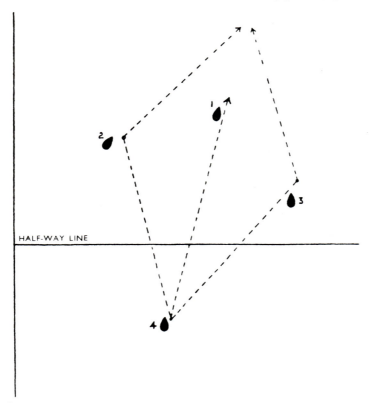

FIG. 24. THE FREE HIT

POSITIONS AT THE HIT-IN

Figure 25 (on the next page) shows the hit-in, the positions of the side hitting in being shown in *black*.

Normally, 3 should hit in, unless the Back is a much stronger hitter. He should follow-up his own shot at a gallop. It will be seen that the suggested position for the Back is on the 30-yard line where he can interfere with the opposing 1 meeting the ball.

The ball should normally be hit-in in such a way that 2, by starting to gallop from the 30-yard line as soon as it is struck, can pick it up on his off-side near the boards. The direction should be varied slightly; otherwise

SPECIMEN ORGANISATION

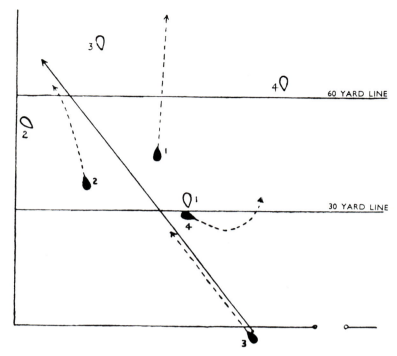

FIG. 25. OWN HIT-IN

the opponents will come to know how the ball will be hit. If 1 is unmarked and 2 is being interfered with, the ball can be hit more towards the centre for 1 to pick up; but this is a dangerous place for the ball to be in if anything should miscarry.

Occasionally the player about to hit-in may warn his fellow-back to move over to the opposite side of goal unobtrusively; he can then hit across the goal to him. If the opponents are caught napping, the Back can get well away; but his failure to pick up the ball in this case will probably give the enemy a free shot at goal.

If the striker can be counted on to hit a long, lofted ball, the forwards should start from beyond the 60-yard line and the fellow-back should be well beyond the 30-yard line and on the opposite side of the goal so that the striker may be free to hit to whichever of the other three players is in the best position to take the ball on unmarked. When the ball is hit across to the fellow-back the striker must follow up hard; 2 turns and plays in the position of Back, 1 going right up for a pass as usual. With a good striker this organisation for the hit-in is unbeatable and strongly recommended.

SPECIMEN ORGANISATION
SPECIAL EXAMPLES

When the ball is cleared out into a corner from the enemy goal, 1 always remains in the centre; and Number 2 should gallop out to the boards and centre the ball with a backhander. If Number 2 is obviously unable to do this, however, either 3 or 4 must gallop out to the ball instead.

Whichever player goes out to the boards must not waste time in coming back into the game. The moment he has centred the ball, he must turn, ride back, and assume the Back-position, so that the other three players can keep up the attack in front of goal.

When the player to do this is Number 2, 3 will take his place and 4 will become temporary 3, the readjustment taking place later in the ordinary way.

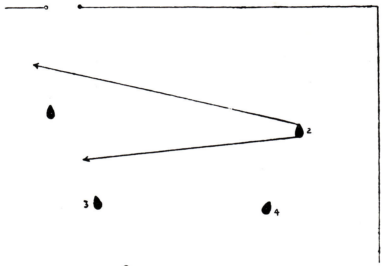

FIG. 26. ATTACK FROM THE BOARDS

If, in the course of the game, one of the forwards should have to take the ball up the boards, owing to the disposition of opponents between him and the enemy goal, one of the Backs must gallop up and lie clear for a pass. For if the player in possession sees that his fellow-forward (who will of course have gone right up-field as usual) is being closely marked by the enemy Back, he will have to centre it with a backhander, and it is essential that there should be someone in position to receive the ball.

If 3 is the one to gallop up, 4 will have to back up the player in possession; and if the latter should be ridden over the ball, 4 will have to take it himself and centre it to 3. (See Figure 26.)

If 3 should be the player to take the ball up the boards, however, it is

SPECIMEN ORGANISATION

2 that must go into position for a backhand centre; and 4 will again back the player in possession of the ball.

Taking the ball up the boards, however, is to be avoided as much as possible. You should avoid everything that wastes time, and slows up your attack.

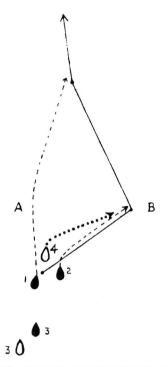

FIG. 27. TWO PLAYERS ON THE BALL

Occasionally, two players on the same side arrive simultaneously on the ball. Figure 27 illustrates the case when black 1 and 2 have got bunched together on the ball.

In the unlikely event of 3, coming up from behind, being unmarked, he should shout, 'Leave it': upon which 1 and 2 will gallop outwards to A and B respectively, one of them drawing the opposing Back. Then 3 can either go through himself, if it is near goal, or pass to whichever forward is free. If no call to leave the ball is made, and there is no one ahead of the two bunched players, to take a pass, the one nearer enemy goal (in this case 2) must immediately gallop wide of the enemy Back, to B; while 1 hits to 2 and then gallops on up past A. If the Back goes with 1 (instead of with 2, as shown in the figure), 2 will have an open goal in front of him.

SPECIMEN ORGANISATION

When attacking, you may suddenly find yourself in possession of the ball, being at the same time the player on your side nearest to the enemy goal, and with the enemy Back nearer his goal than you are.

Figure 28 shows a typical case. This is a situation most likely to occur shortly after an enemy attack has been stopped; otherwise your Number 1 should not have allowed the opposing Back to get between him and the enemy goal.

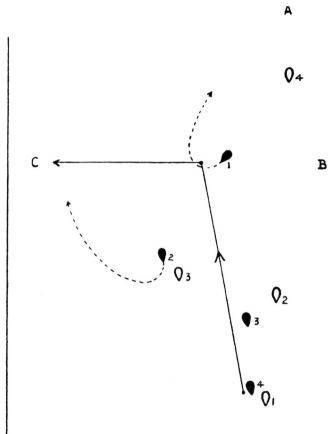

FIG. 28. MAN NEAREST ENEMY GOAL IN POSSESSION

Don't hit blindly in the direction of goal (A).

If you hit towards the centre (B in the figure), you will merely have to race the enemy 2 for the next shot. If you leave it, the enemy Back will get the ball. You must either hold it till one of your side has turned; or else, better, hit it to such a position that one of your side can get there first. Although hitting to C involves a stroke in almost the opposite direction to

101

SPECIMEN ORGANISATION

enemy goal (A), it will enable 2 to pick up the ball and is therefore best in the circumstances. You should turn up as you hit it, and gallop up for 2's pass, or take the enemy Back out of 2's way. If there is any doubt, call the name of the player to whom you intend to pass; unless, of course, the player who could take a pass calls for one first. The important thing is to retain possession at all costs for your own side; and in this case you would do better to pass in the wrong direction (C), than to lose possession by hitting in what is normally the right one.

But this is the 'exception that proves the rule'.

DEFENCE

The best form of defence is attack. Don't become resigned to the game's going against you, but always be on the look-out to turn back your opponents, and reorganise yourselves in attack-formation. You should remain attackers, even when the ball is travelling in the direction of your own goal, by interfering with and harrying your opponents.

Go hard for your man. Never let him take a shot unmarked through having tried to make certain of cutting him off before he could take a second: for if his first shot is a pass, there probably will be no second shot for you to prevent! Even if he were actually intending to place a first shot for his own second shot, it would be unpardonable that you should allow the amount of ground to be lost that delaying your interference would entail.

When you are a forward, and in defence, never feel tempted not to ride your man actively because the ball is not near you, and you see that it is among your own backs. If the enemy Back stays well out of the game and is not well covered, he will be able to come through at full speed; and you will find it pretty difficult to pick up a passing opponent that has started galloping hard, without warning, from twenty yards behind you.

Just as you must be ready to get away in attack-formation from the moment the ball comes into play, so, if your opponents should get hold of the ball first, you must at once get into defence-formation.

POSITIONS AT THE THROW-IN

At the throw-in, if opposing 1, 2, or 3 meets the ball, the corresponding number on your side, who is marking him, must ride him hard and stick to him until his attack is stopped.

SPECIMEN ORGANISATION

It is obvious that, the moment the ball passes a player and his corresponding opponent, he must begin to do the same thing without waiting to see who gets the ball.

Number 1 must push his way round in front of his opposing Number 1, impeding his progress, and then he must go straight to the enemy Back, or temporary Back, if the enemy still retains possession of the ball. If his side regains possession, he must go up forward for a pass, as usual. In going up to the enemy Back, he must in any case be on the look-out for a pass from 3 (see Figure 29).

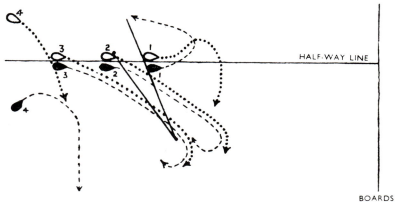

FIG. 29. OPPONENTS MEETING THE BALL AT THE THROW-IN

Number 2 must ride off his opposing Number 2. Number 3 goes to the ball, and tries to backhander it up to his forwards. If it goes past him at the throw-in, he must turn to cover his own Back.

If the Back, after racing for the ball with the enemy Back, should fail to get it, the team is faced with a particularly dangerous situation. As this takes him right out of the game, one of the opposing side must obviously be unmarked; since the defending Number 1 will have turned into the enemy half to mark the opposing Back (and since this is the player who has galloped through), the chances are that both the defending 1 and defending Back will be temporarily out of the game, leaving two opponents free. Heroic measures will be needed to save the situation. Number 3, who should in any case have turned towards his goal, must now spare no effort to take the ball away from the attacking Back; whilst 2 now takes on the next most dangerous opponent. Defending 1 and Back must close as quickly as possible with the remaining two.

SPECIMEN ORGANISATION

POSITIONS AT THE HIT-IN

Positions for the defending side at the enemy hit-in are shown in *black* in Figure 30.

Numbers 1, 2, and 3 should cover between them the most likely shots; if the opposing striker generally hits more towards the middle of the ground than the positions in Figure 30 cater for, 1, 2 and 3 must adjust their

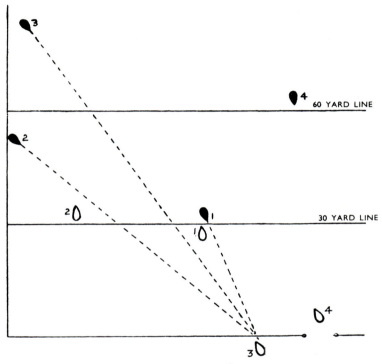

FIG. 30. OPPONENTS' HIT-IN

positions accordingly. Number 1 should be crossing the 30-yard line at a gallop just as the ball is being hit or hit at, as this will disconcert the enemy hitter-in and prevents him from tapping first without the risk of losing possession. Numbers 2 and 3, especially the latter, should both start from a long way back if the striker is known to hit a long ball, as this gives them more chance of meeting it. The player meeting the ball should first move quickly across to the line it has been hit on and then gallop down this line (for this will give him equal possession with anyone riding to meet him on exactly the same line), taking care to take the ball on the off-side, as laid down in Field Rule 16 (a) (ii).

SPECIMEN ORGANISATION

Number 3 must be ready to turn back in defence and to hit a backhander, if an opponent should pick up the ball.

The Back must stay in the centre to deal with a hit down the centre of the ground or across the goal. The first player to notice that such a shot is about to be made should shout to warn his side and enable them to move across and counter it.

POSITIONS AT THE 30-YARD, 40-YARD, 60-YARD AND FREE HITS

Figure 22 on page 95 shows the 40-yard hit; positions of the fouling side being shown in *outline*. The positions for the 30-yard hit are similar for the fouling side, but the hit will be taken from the 30-yard line.

The inner positions should be occupied by the players that are best at meeting the ball.

Figure 23 shows the 60-yard hit; positions of the fouling side being shown in *outline*.

Number 1 should be as close to the ball as he is allowed to be: that is to say, thirty yards away. The Back should be on the goal-line, and must shout, 'Let it go,' if he sees that the shot is obviously going wide.

It is essential that all the players on the fouling side should be between the ball and their own goal, so as to offer the greatest possible obstruction.

For a free hit, much the same positions should be taken up as for a 60-yard hit, provided that all the opponents, except the striker, be properly marked.

INFORMATIVE CALLING

Informative calling, as you were told in Chapter 5, must be sparingly used.

The first important consideration is that every call made in the game must be made for a good reason. A call for a pass, for instance, must be made because the caller can advantageously receive the ball; and a call for the ball to be left must be made only because the player in possession would obviously do better to gallop up and mark the enemy, or else because the caller has a 'sitting' shot at goal.

The second important consideration in informative calling is that every call must be shouted loud and clear, so that it can be heard by a man galloping at full speed with his attention fully occupied. A good loud shout, as a matter of fact, will have the additional advantage of commanding instinctive obedience, and making the other player react quickly.

SPECIMEN ORGANISATION

The third important consideration is that the words used should be easy to distinguish, and that their meaning should be certain. No words should be used that are difficult to enunciate clearly, loud; and no expressions should be used that could bear a double meaning. If you shout 'Go on,' for instance, you are inviting the player to guess whether you mean 'go on; hit the ball,' or 'go on; and leave the ball for me.' In order to avoid the words being misheard, therefore, or their meaning being misinterpreted, you will have to codify the expressions used, so that they become the agreed conventions of the team.

LIST OF CALLS

The following is the list of calls suggested for a specimen organisation:

>Take the ball;
>Leave it;
>Turn;
>Gallop up;
>Go back;
>Lots of time;
>Let it go;

and the name of the player to whom the call is addressed.

Take the Ball

It must be clear that this is not an optional call. The player addressed must strike the ball, however badly placed he may be, and however well placed he may imagine the caller to be.

You cannot know that the player you think most advantageously placed may not that moment have broken his stick, for instance, so you must never hesitate to obey.

Leave it

The player addressed must instantly leave the ball, even if his stroke is already half made.

Don't forget that this call implies also, 'get out of the line of fire, and ride the nearest man well out of the way.'

Turn

This call, usually addressed to the whole team (e.g. 'Turn Bluejackets'), is used more in practice than in match-play, till such time as the forwards

SPECIMEN ORGANISATION

have learnt to keep a look-out over their shoulders in attack, and the backs a similar look-out in defence.

Gallop up

This call to the whole team is useful when the team is still in training; and is intended to make the forwards go well up in attack, as well as to stop them from turning back when they miss the ball, and one of the backs is there to meet it.

When the team improves, the occasions for its use will gradually disappear; particularly when the forwards learn to look back over their shoulders frequently, to see what is going on behind them.

This call will remain of use when addressed to a particular player to indicate that he should move 'up' towards the enemy goal.

Go back

This call tells a player to move 'back' towards his own goal.

Lots of Time

This call is used when a player is approaching the enemy goal with the ball, and has not realised that he has shaken off pursuit and need not hurry over his stroke.

Let it go

This call is useful for telling a player, who is about to take a back-hander, that he can safely let the ball go over the line, since it is not in danger of going through his goal: for he may not have noticed this, through keeping his eye on the ball for his stroke.

If he lets the ball go, he must stay with it, however, to prevent any opponent from reaching it before it has crossed the back line.

Calling by Name for a Pass

The best way to call for a pass is to call the player in possession by name; for the sound of your voice will tell him what direction to pass in, whatever words you use, and no expression is likely to attract his attention so quickly as his own name will. In the same way, the player in possession can make it clear to whom he wishes to pass the ball, by shouting the name of the player he intends to hit to.

SPECIMEN ORGANISATION

CONSIDERATIONS OF PONY-POWER

The question of pony-power is of the first importance in tournament play.

In drawing-up a plan for using the pony-power of his team to the greatest advantage, the captain will be faced with two or three problems simultaneously.

He will have to decide in which chukkas he wants the team to be best mounted. He must then decide which players shall be well enough mounted in the remaining chukkas, to cover any weakness of their adjacent players; and how these objects can be combined with the periods of rest necessary for the ponies.

The captain should warn the team of which chukka he has allowed to become the weakest, so that they may play with extra care. The weakest chukka should be altered, so that observant opponents, whom the team has already played, shall not benefit from their previous experience.

If the team know the ponies they are up against, they should try and bring out a fast pony when their opposite number is on a fast pony (having obtained the captain's approval beforehand). The captain may even order changes of this kind himself.

Before a match he must get each member of the team to submit the order in which they propose to play their ponies. With due regard to this list, he must then make the changes necessary. If he considers that the order of importance of the chukkas is:

> Last chukka but one;
> first chukka;
> last chukka;

he will have to see to it that the whole team are on their best ponies in the penultimate chukka, and try to dispose the ponies to the best advantage in the remaining ones.

The last chukka but one is usually the most important, and many closely contested games appear to hinge on it. A team that either catches up in this chukka and establishes a lead, or else manages to consolidate an existing lead, should be able to maintain this, or even improve on it, in the last chukka (unless they have only their worst ponies left, to play on).

In four-chukka matches, as a matter of fact, owing to the short duration of play, the last chukka is probably equally important; but in ordinary full-length matches this will rarely be the case.

SPECIMEN ORGANISATION

The importance of being well mounted in the first chukka is largely a psychological one. By enabling individual players to hit the ball more easily at the beginning, since they are not on troublesome ponies, it gives them a confidence which is reflected in the play of the team as a whole, and gets the team going well together from the start.

In most cases a player will have a definite order of preference for his ponies, depending chiefly on the feeling that he plays better on one than on another. He should put his ponies down in his order of preference, and give it to the captain. Let us call these ponies A, B, C, D, etc. . . .

Before each match he should also prepare a list showing which chukkas he wishes to play his ponies in. The captain then combines the lists. In teams that pool their ponies his task will be greatly simplified.

A typical organisation for a six-chukka match is shown in the table below. The players are assumed to have four ponies each; with the exception of Number 1, who has only three ponies. When 1 is on his worst pony, C, 2 plays his best, A, in the second chukka. Number 2 cannot conveniently play this pony again in the fourth chukka; but he can at any rate arrange ponies to avoid playing his worst pony, D, in the same chukka. The Back can arrange to play his difficult pony, D, while his No. 3 is on a good pony, B; and while 3 is on a fast but rather unmanageable pony, D, the Back brings out a very reliable though slow pony, C.

Chukka No.	No. 1 (3 ponies)	No. 2 (4 ponies)	No. 3 (4 ponies)	Back (4 ponies)
1	A	B	A	A
2	C	A	B	D
3	B	D	C	B
4	C	C	D	C
5	A	A	A	A
6	B	B	B	B

The question of spare ponies is also important. One pony per player must be girthed up and ready for play, standing by in case he should be suddenly needed. If a curb-hook draws, a stirrup-leather breaks, or a pony goes lame, it is vital to reduce the time the player concerned is out of action to the minimum possible. Unless a player has so many ponies that he can afford to have one as spare all the way through a game, the simplest rule will be to have the 'next pony out' standing by as spare the chukka before

SPECIMEN ORGANISATION

he is due to play. This is obviously impossible when a player has only two ponies; for the one that has just played must be rubbed down when he comes in, and cannot be left girthed up as a spare.

The captain should make it clear that, if the team is not down by more than three goals or so, at the end of a certain chukka, he expects to win. This will be encouraging to them if the score should be against them until that chukka.

When things are going badly the tide can often be turned by the whole team getting on their best ponies for one chukka. But over-confidence should not make them (possibly without consulting the captain) bring out bad ponies for the last chukka, in order to save their good ones for the next match, and risk being 'beaten at the post'.

APPENDICES

APPENDIX I

STABLE MANAGEMENT

Though you may have started polo on hirelings, you will find that a new enjoyment comes to you with the acquisition of your first pony. The fact of ownership will provide you with a real interest on non-polo days as well as when you are playing; and you are sure to want to know how your pony is being looked after, and to take part in looking after him.

The following appendix does not set out to supply sufficient information to enable you to run your own stable; but is intended to give you a nucleus on which to build up gradually, through your own observation and experience, a knowledge of stable management. Several excellent books on this subject are listed in the Bibliography at the end of this book, and you are advised to read them if you want to learn how to run your own stable. Meanwhile, there is no reason why the average pony should not be maintained at full efficiency, or even improved, if you see to it that great attention is paid to the points that are gone into below.

CONDITION

Your pony's condition (*i.e.* physical fitness) will depend to a great extent on good stable management; that is to say, on healthy exercise, good grooming, careful watering and feeding; and on decent treatment, which makes for a contented mind.

If you have no experience of stable management, you must accustom yourself to consider your pony as a reasonable and responsive creature: treat him intelligently, and you will not go far wrong.

A fit pony can be recognised by the following signs:

Body: muscular and well furnished (*i.e.* well covered with flesh and muscle but carrying no belly).

Skin: bright and supple (*i.e.* not tight to the ribs, but so that a handful of it can be caught hold of).

Eye, bright.

Appetite: good (*i.e.* he should always be ready for his food; although some ponies will always be dainty feeders and will not try to swallow the whole feed at once).

Droppings: fairly firm and not slimy.

Body: warm.

Legs and feet: cold.

EXERCISE

A pony being prepared for playing needs to be walked and slowly trotted up and down hill for three hours daily, to build up his muscles. (No pony with the

APPENDIX I

weight of a man on his back should at any time be called upon, or allowed, to trot fast; for this will jar his joints unduly.)

Two hours of exercise are usually given in the morning, between first and second feeds; and another hour in the afternoon.

During the afternoon exercise, knock about with stick and ball at a canter for five minutes, increasing progressively to ten minutes; this will gradually get the pony fit. But it is the long, slow trot for four miles at a time, up and down hill, that really does the work.

When once your pony is fit, and playing five or six chukkas a week, one hour of walking and trotting every day will keep him in condition.

After a hard tournament, half-an-hour to three-quarters of an hour of being led around, on the following day, should be enough to remove any stiffness.

GROOMING

A pony in a stable, being fed on grain, needs to be groomed as well as exercised.

His grooming should be thorough, strenuous, and quick.

One good grooming every week is better than a 'lick and a promise' every day; but the pony should really be properly groomed once a day. In order to satisfy yourself that he is properly groomed and clean, pay attention to the following points:

Pick up all his feet and see that they are clean inside, and that the frog (see Figure 1) is healthy and free from any bad smell. The latter is often caused by a disease called 'thrush'.

See that his eyes, nose and dock have been sponged out.

Rub your fingers against the hair in places that are awkward to get at, such as under the throat, inside the elbow, the point of the hock, the knee, etc.

Watch the horse stale (*i.e.* pass water). If his penis or sheath is dirty, it should be washed with warm water and soap.

WATERING

A pony needs from five to fifteen gallons of water every day.

He should either be watered before every feed, or, better, have a bucket of water always in front of him. But in the latter case, the bucket must be taken away three hours before a game.

The more water a healthy pony will drink, the better; but he must never be watered after feeding. It will be found, as a matter of fact, that a pony often takes a short drink after feeding when the bucket is left in the stable; but the quantity taken in these cases is invariably too small to be detrimental.

FEEDING

A pony has a small stomach, and should therefore be fed frequently and in small amounts.

Feed your pony at least four times a day; five or six times is even better.

STABLE MANAGEMENT

Feed him, as far as possible, at regular times, and both as early and as late as is feasible: in this way, he will have to go for as short a period as possible during the night with an empty stomach.

A fifteen-hand pony can be kept in hard playing condition on 12 lbs. of grain (usually oats), and a daily allowance of 12 lbs. of hay.

Oats, which in England are the normal grain, play the part that meat plays in a man's diet, and helps to build and keep up muscle. Bran can be substituted for grain, as required. (Hay acts as a bulk, but is not very nutritious.)

If a man overfeeds on meat, his blood goes wrong and he breaks out in spots: too much corn will have the same effect on a pony, and will often cause him to get out of condition. Just as a man can cure this by taking Eno's or a pill, so can a pony be cured by a purge, such as Epsom salts or a physic ball. A cupiss ball can be given if a mild laxative is required.

Bran is a fat-making food, and can be given mixed with oats. It is an extremely useful regulator. If your pony is purging, dry bran will help to bind; whereas if he is tight of his coat and bound, wet bran will act as a laxative.

It is a good plan to give a pony a bran-mash once a week (usually on Saturday nights), and to leave him in the stable the whole of the following day. A bran-mash for one animal is made by pouring from two to three lbs. of dry bran into about one gallon and a half of boiling water, and stirring until the bran is saturated. The mash should then be allowed to cool, after which from six to eight ounces of linseed (which must previously have been soaked for twenty-four hours and then boiled for one hour) may be added, together with from two to four ounces of Epsom salts. This should be given instead of the last feed at night.

Bran-mash acts as a laxative. Without Epsom salts, it is a mild laxative only; and being more easily digestible may be given without them after a hard match.

When possible, chaff (chopped hay) should be added to the grain in each feed; and the two should be mixed together with salt water, in order to damp them, before they are put in the manger. In addition to the kitchen salt, which is used in mixing, a block of rock salt, if procurable, should be kept in the manger.

A reasonable scale of feeding for a pony in England is:

    6.0 a.m.   2 lbs. of grain, 1 lb chaff
   10.30 a.m. 3 ,, ,, 1 ,, ,,
    2.0 p.m.   2 ,, ,, 1 ,, ,,
    5.0 p.m.   2 ,, ,, 1 ,, ,,
    8.0 p.m.   3 ,, ,, 1 ,, ,,
   Total: 12 lbs. of grain; 5 lbs. of chaff.

This leaves seven pounds of hay to put down, of which 2 lbs. can be given while the pony is being groomed, and 5 lbs. after the last feed at night. Alternatively, the whole 7 lbs. can be given at night.

On a polo-playing day, the pony must miss the 2 p.m. feed, as he should not be fed within five hours of being required to play fast polo. The other feeds must be increased accordingly. (Cantering games do not matter, provided that one hour be left between feeding and playing.)

APPENDIX I

Give your pony a variety of feed whenever you can, as this will help to keep his blood in good order.

Linseed is good for the coat, but heating to the blood.

Green food is good, both for the blood and coat.

Boiled grain is fattening, and therefore excellent for a thin pony; but it is also rather softening.

If a pony eats his straw bedding he should be muzzled, or else his bedding should be changed to peat-moss or sawdust.

THE CONTENTED MIND

A pony hates noise, and being shouted at; or having another pony to lean over and try to eat out of his manger.

He will always hate a noisy, bad-tempered groom; but will appreciate the quiet attentions of someone considerate and understanding.

If your pony is doing badly, stand unobtrusively in the stable for half-an-hour during his feeding-time. This may afford you a chance to discover what is the matter. Perhaps his teeth are too sharp; perhaps he is bolting his feed; or perhaps he is worried by other ponies, or frightened of his groom.

Make your pony as comfortable as you can.

Remember that a pony in a stall is compelled to look at one patch of wall for twenty hours out of every twenty-four, so if you can put your pony in a loose-box, instead, you should do so.

When your pony is in a box, don't tie him up, but encourage him to lie down as much as possible.

Keep him warm. Draughts, particularly on his legs, are bad for him. But a stuffy atmosphere, of course, must also be avoided.

CARE OF MOUTH

Get someone experienced to show you how to examine a pony's teeth (see Figure 1); and every day your pony plays, examine his mouth yourself.

Cuts usually occur on the inside of the bars, about one inch below the bottom molar. A pony with a cut bar can never play his best, and the cut will not heal if you continue to play him in any bit that acts on the bars of the mouth. Until the cut is healed, try a running-rein on a snaffle, as the latter does not act on the bars of the mouth, but on the lips.

When the pony has a cut mouth, wash it after he has played, and after every feed. The best cure, if it can be arranged, is to turn the pony out to grass for about a week.

If you cut the inside of your pony's lips when playing (probably with the snaffle of a double bridle, or more often with a gag), see if this is due to the bottom molars being sharp. Play him in a bit without a snaffle (*e.g.* a Pelham) until the cut is healed.

Some ponies have a mouth too small to hold a double bridle with comfort; others hate a Pelham; and so on ...

STABLE MANAGEMENT

You must, therefore, keep on experimenting until you are certain that your pony is really comfortably bitted.

HEALTH

Remember that a pony can only tell you he is unwell by refusing his feed; or by kicking, and looking at his stomach, which he will do if he has colic. If he refuses to feed, always have his temperature taken at once, unless there is some obvious reason (*e.g.* injured mouth, etc.) for his behaviour.

If you find that oats are being passed whole in dung, it will be obvious to you that they are not being ground by the molars. The reason for this may be that the pony's teeth are sharp, and that it is hurting him to grind; or else, it may be he is merely bolting his feed. If the teeth are sharp, they should be rasped.

There are few minor ailments that cannot be cured by the intelligent application of hot or cold water, according to the injury. A bottle of disinfectant and a tin of antiphlogistine should always be at hand; the latter will save your groom the time he would otherwise spend in preparing fomentations.

Feel the pony's tendons, ligaments, and joints every day. In this way you will know when heat first comes to some part of a leg, and be able to apply treatment before any serious trouble develops.

After he has played on a hard ground, your pony's legs may fill and become puffy. This can be obviated by the use of some kind of leg preparation. Of these, there are a great many, but the local vet. will probably be able to give you a suitable prescription. Failing this, you will find whitening, mixed into a paste with vinegar and smeared on the tendon, efficacious.

Insist that your groom trot the pony up every morning following play, and report any lameness to you at once.

If your pony is lame, and you suspect the lameness to be in the foot, always have the shoe off, and see that the foot is examined by the farrier.

If his hind-legs swell up at night, it is hardly ever due to work, but usually to his being out of condition. This can in most cases be put right by a dose of physic.

When a pony goes lame and has to be kept in, put him on soft food by substituting wet bran for half of his grain.

If a pony sustains an injury, even severe, to muscle, joint or ligament the most rapid and complete recovery will be obtained when treated by Rythmic Muscular Contractions. This system, based on sound physiological principles, exercises the muscle of the injured area and those working on and over the injured part, by using the S.E.V.A., specially designed for the purpose (see page 14). It should be applied as soon as possible immediately following the injury. This increases the circulation both to and from the injured part. The latter is very important as no other known treatment achieves this to the same extent. The process of healing is vastly improved and the movement created prevents the formation of adhesions, which, if formed, might eventually be as crippling as the original injury if it is treated by over-rest, heat, bandaging or anti-inflammatory drugs. If these injuries are treated by S.E.V.A. using the correct technique, in all detail from the earliest moment experience has shown that this avoids the injuries becoming chronic.

APPENDIX I

SHOEING

See that your pony has good calkins in his hind shoes. Screw calkins, which are allowed by the Field Rules, are the best, for when worn down they can be replaced without new shoes having to be fitted. Ponies doing road-work need shoeing about every three weeks, whilst calkins wear down in seven to ten days.

You can no more expect a pony to play well, without good calkins, than you could yourself expect to play tennis well on a grass court in flat leather soles. The calkins help him to stop; for if he slips in stopping or turning, he will not be able to do it correctly (*i.e.* by using his hind legs as brakes), but will 'prop' with his forelegs. This will give you a bad ride, and will get your pony into bad habits.

AT POLO

If your pony is to play in more than one chukka in any match he must be well rubbed down between chukkas. On a cold day rubbing down with a dry rubber is enough, but if he is sweating, and it is a warm day with no risk of his catching a chill, he should also be washed.

A good groom can do this thoroughly in five minutes, and if done really well it will make all the difference to the pony's freshness in his next chukka.

First of all his mouth should be washed out with a spongeful of fresh water; and his brow-band should be slipped back, so that he can be sponged all round behind the ears. Then the saddle should be taken off, and he should be washed down all over with a wet sponge, scraped off, and wiped dry with a chamois-leather or stable rubber. Next he should be rubbed down well with a dry stable rubber; and the saddle should be put on again, but the girths left slack. And finally, he should be covered: usually a summer sheet is used for this, but on cold, windy days a rug is better. Best of all is a Jaeger 'cooler'; but these are expensive.

WINTERING IN ENGLAND

At the end of the polo season, 'rough-up' your pony for three or four days; that is to say, don't have him groomed, and stop feeding him corn.

Give him a physic; and as soon as he has got over this, take off his shoes and turn him out to grass, for the winter. If there is nourishment in the grass, he need not be fed while he is out; but if the grass is poor he should have about 3 lbs. of oats every evening.

If the weather turns very cold, you may find that your pony does better in a roomy loose-box than he would out of doors. Feed him hay, and about 2 lbs. of oats a day. When he is 'roughed-up' like this, he need not be exercised or groomed.

When your pony is finally 'brought-up' from grass, he should again be given a physic, in order to clear the grass out of his system; and after recovering from this, he should be on full feed and full exercise for at least two months before he can be expected to play fast polo.

APPENDIX II

HISTORY OF THE RULES

THE first Rules of Polo in the English language were drawn up at a meeting of the Silchar Kangjai Club in India on 1st January, 1863. These rules were very different from the present-day ones as may be judged from two examples:

RULE 20. Spurs and whips may be freely used, but only on the rider's own horse; to beat an adversary's horse is foul play.

RULE 22. It is to be understood that no player shall be under the influence of spirituous liquor.

The first Polo Club in England to produce Rules of Polo was the Monmouthshire Polo Club, who published them in April, 1873. The Hurlingham Club Rules of Polo were published two years later on May 12th, 1875, and annually ever since with such changes as experience has shown to be necessary, until 1939, when they were embodied in the International Rules.

In March, 1892, the Indian Polo Association was formed, and issued the Rules of Polo to govern play all over India. These rules were in general agreement with the well established Hurlingham Rules, as were the first rules issued by other associations such as the United States Polo Association, who first issued their Rules in 1890. Thus in the early days of the game players all over the world played under rules which were almost identical in wording and arrangement.

The various polo associations, however, gradually changed the wording and eventually even some of the 'numbers' of their rules and penalties. By 1938 there were considerable differences between the rules in use in the United States, in India and in those countries which played under the Hurlingham Rules.

In 1938 the Chairman of the Hurlingham Rules Committee (the Chairman was actually the Author of this book) met the Chairman of the United States Polo Association, as a result of which an 'International Rules Committee' was set up under the Chairmanship of the former, to which all other Polo Associations, who published their own rules, were invited to appoint representatives. A set of International Rules of Polo was drawn up by The Hurlingham Polo Association Committee, which endeavoured to meet as far as possible the desires of the various Polo Associations. The aim was to have similar numbers and wording universally and to clarify loosely worded rules (such as Field Rule 16 on Crossing), but changing the actual rules as little as possible, except for the introduction of the new idea of stopping each period when the ball was in a neutral position.

All Polo Associations adopted the new rules in principle, except the U.S.P.A., although their rules were substantially the same, the numbering of some of the rules was different. The International Rules of Polo remained in force in England until 1965, when, largely owing to visitors from other countries who wished to play with some

APPENDIX II

changes made in their own countries, the 'International Rules of Polo' were changed to the 'Hurlingham Polo Association Rules of Polo'. These actually differed little from the International Rules, but under them all Commonwealth and foreign visitors played in England without argument.

The following Commonwealth and other countries play under these Hurlingham Polo Association Rules, and also have representatives on the Hurlingham Polo Association Council: The Polo Associations of Australia, New Zealand, India, Pakistan, South Africa, Rhodesia, Malta, Cyprus, Kenya, Nigeria, Malaysia, Hong Kong, Jamaica, Zambia, Singapore and Ghana. Overseas Clubs playing under Hurlingham Association Rules are, Country Club Diplomatique, Tangier; Dusseldorf Polo Club; Hamburg Polo Club; Barbados Polo Club and the Royal Jordan Polo Club. These Clubs are without council representation.

APPENDIX III
THE HURLINGHAM POLO ASSOCIATION RULES OF POLO
INDEX

GENERAL RULES

		PAGE
1.	Height of Ponies	122
2.	Size of Grounds	122
3.	Size of Ball	122
4.	Qualifications of Players	122
5.	Umpires, Referees and Goal Judges	123
6.	Timekeeper and Scorer	123
7.	Duration of Play and Handicap Allowances	123
8.	How A Game is Won	125
9.	Polo Helmet or Cap	125
10.	Confusing Colours	125

FIELD RULES

1.	Definition of Foul	125
2.	Dead Ball	125
3.	Disqualified Ponies	125
4.	Equipment for Ponies	125
5.	Disqualified Equipment for Players	125
6.	Safety Zone	126
7.	Start of Game	126
8.	How A Goal is Scored	126
9.	Changing of Ends	126
10.	Attackers Hit Behind	126
11.	Defenders Hit Behind	126
12.	Ball Hit Out	127
13.	Restarting after Interval	127
14.	Damaged Ball	127
15.	Carrying the Ball	127
16.	Crossing	127
17.	Dangerous Riding	129
18.	Rough Handling	129
19.	Misuse of Stick	129

		PAGE
20.	Loss of Headgear	129
21.	Dismounted Player	129
22.	Accident or Injury	129
23.	Disablement	130
24.	When Game is Not Stopped	130
25.	Restarting When Ball Was Not Out	130
26.	Discretion of Umpires	130

PENALTIES

1.	Penalty Goal	130
2.	30-Yard Hit	130
3.	40-Yard Hit	131
4.	60-Yard Hit (Opposite Goal)	131
5.	Free Hit (a) From Spot	131
5.	Free Hit (b) From Centre	131
6.	60-yard Hit (Opposite Where Ball Crossed)	131
7.	(a) Another Hit	131
	(b) Hit in by Defenders	131
	(c) Hit in from 30-Yard Line	131
	(d) Unneccessary Delay	132
8.	Player to Retire	132
9.	(a) Pony Disqualified	132
	(b) Pony Ordered Off	132
	(c) Player Ordered Off	132
10.	Player Excluded	132

FIELD RULES 16 & 17

I.	16 (f), 16 (g), and 16 (c) (iv)	133
II.	16 (c) (i), and 16 (a) (i)	134
III.	16 (e) (i), and 16 (g)	135
IV.	16 (c) (iii)	136
V.	16 (c) (ii)	137
VI.	16 (c) (v)	138
VII.	17 (d)	139

APPENDIX III

THE HURLINGHAM POLO ASSOCIATION RULES OF POLO

GENERAL RULES

Height of Ponies. 1.—Ponies of any height may be played.

Size of Grounds. 2.—(*a*) A full-sized ground shall not exceed 300 yards in length by 200 yards in width, if unboarded; and 300 yards in length by 160 yards in width, if boarded.

(*b*) The goals shall not be less than 250 yards apart, and each goal shall be 8 yards wide.

(*c*) The goal posts shall be at least 10 feet high, and light enough to break if collided with.

(*d*) The boards shall not exceed 11 inches in height.

Size of Ball. 3.—The size of the ball shall not exceed $3\frac{1}{2}$ inches in diameter, and the weight of the ball shall be within the limits of $4\frac{1}{4}$ to $4\frac{3}{4}$ ounces.

Qualifications of Players. 4.—(*a*) The number of players is limited to 4 a side in all games and matches.

(*b*) No player shall play with his left hand.

(*c*) A player may be substituted for another during a match only if the latter player through sickness, accident or duty is unable to continue. In such case the handicap of the player having the highest handicap shall be counted, irrespective of the period in which the substitution takes place.

(*d*) If a player, who has taken part in one or more of the earlier rounds of a tournament, is unable, for any reason, to play in a later round or rounds he may be replaced by a substitute. A *bona fide* member of a team, who is, for any reason, unable to play in the earlier rounds of a tournament may also be replaced by a substitute.

(*e*) Unless the Tournament Committee agree that it is expedient for the welfare of the tournament, no player may play for more than one team. There is no such restriction on ponies unless the conditions of the tournament provide otherwise. Substitutes must be qualified to play in the event and the team must remain qualified after the substitution has been made.

(*f*) A Tournament Committee shall not agree to a player who has already played in a team in the tournament playing as a substitute in any other team in that tournament unless:

(i) They consider there is no suitable* player available who has not already played in the tournament.

(ii) They are satisfied that there is a *bona fide* need for a substitute.

(iii) The total handicap of the team requiring a substitute will not be increased thereby.

(iv) In matches with an international flavour the Captain of the opposing side agrees.

H. P. A. GENERAL RULES

Where possible, preference should be given to a player who has been defeated in the first rounds of the tournament.

(*Note.—A player should be regarded as suitable if his handicap is not more than two goals less than the handicap of the player he is replacing.)

5.—(a) The rules shall be administered in a match by two Umpires, who shall be mounted to enable them to keep close to the play, and a Referee who shall remain off the field of play in a central position. By mutual agreement between Captains of teams, one Umpire, and if desired, also the Referee, may be dispensed with. The decision of the Umpire shall be final, except where there are two and they disagree, in which case the decision of the Referee shall be final. **Umpires, Referees and Goal Judges.**

(b) In important matches Goal Judges should be appointed each of whom shall give testimony to the Umpires at the latter's request in respect to goals or other points of the game near his goal, but the Umpires shall make all decisions.

(c) The above Officials shall be nominated by the Committee conducting the tournament or match except in international matches when they shall be mutually agreed upon.

(d) Captains shall have the sole right to discuss with the Umpire or Umpires questions arising during the game. No player shall appeal in any manner to the Umpire or Umpires for fouls. This does not preclude a Captain from discussing any matter with the Umpire.

(e) The authority of the above Officials shall extend from the time the match is due to start until the end of the game. All questions arising at other times may be referred by the Captains to the Committee conducting the tournament or match and its decision shall be final.

6.—An official Timekeeper and Scorer shall be employed in all games and matches. **Timekeeper and Scorer.**

7.—(a) The duration of play is 42 minutes divided into 6 periods of 7 minutes each. The number of minutes played in a period, or periods played in a match, may be reduced by the Committee conducting the tournament or match. In all matches there shall be a half-time interval of 5 minutes. All other intervals between periods shall be of three minutes' duration. **Duration of Play.**

(b) In all matches played under handicap conditions the higher handicapped team shall concede to the lower handicapped team the difference in the handicaps divided by six and multiplied by the number of periods of play of the match. All fractions of a goal shall count as 'half-a-goal'. Mistakes in handicaps or in computing goal allowances must be challenged before a match begins, and no objection can be entertained afterwards. **Handicap Calculation.**

(c) With the exception of the said intervals, play shall be continuous, and no time shall be taken off for changing ponies during a period, except as legislated for in Field Rule 22. **Play Continuous.**

(d) Each period of play, except the last, shall terminate after the expiration of the prescribed time (designated by the ringing of the bell or other signal) as soon as the ball goes out of play or hits the boards. **Termination of Period.**

A bell or other signal will be sounded 30 seconds after the first bell or signal, if the ball is still in play, and the period will terminate at the first sound of the second bell or other signal, although the ball is still in play, wherever the ball may be.

APPENDIX III

Penalty Exacted Next Period.
(e) If a foul is given after the first stroke of the 7 minute bell, the Umpire's whistle terminates the period, and the penalty shall be exacted at the beginning of the next period, except in the event of a tie in the last period when the penalty shall be exacted at once, and the period continued until the ball goes out of play or hits the boards or the 30 seconds bell is sounded.

Game Stopped.
(f) The game can be stopped in two different ways:
  (i) Where the time during which the game is stopped is *not* to be counted as part of the playing time of the period (i.e. where the clock is to be stopped). To indicate this to the Timekeeper the Umpire should blow one firm blast. This way is used for fouls, Penalty 7 and under Field Rules 11, 14, 20 and 22. The ball is dead until the Umpire says 'Play' and the ball is hit or hit at.
  (ii) Where the time during which the game is stopped is to be counted as part of the playing time of the period (i.e. where the clock is *not* to be stopped). This occurs when the ball goes out of play, through the goal or over the boards, side or back lines (unless hit over the back line by a defender). As a rule the game will automatically stop, but if it continues (e.g. if the ball is hit straight back into play after crossing the back or side lines), the Umpire should blow two sharp blasts. This will tell the Timekeeper not to deduct time.

Last Period.
(g) The last period shall terminate although the ball is still in play, at the first stroke of the 7 minute bell, wherever the ball may be, except in the case of a tie.

(h) In the case of a tie the last period shall be prolonged till the ball goes out of play or hits the boards, or till the 30 seconds bell rings, and if still a tie, after an interval of five minutes the game shall be started from where the ball went out of play and be continued in periods of the usual duration, with the usual intervals, until one side obtains a goal, which shall determine the match.

Widened Goals.
(i) In the event of a tie at the end of the final period of a match goals will be widened for the ensuing periods:
  (i) If the tournament conditions state that this will be so, or
  (ii) If the captains of both teams concerned request that they should be.

In any event goals will be widened if no goal has been scored by the end of the first period of extra time.

Rules for Widened Goals:
  (i) Width of goals to be doubled to 16 yards by moving goal posts 4 yards outwards.
  (ii) After a five minutes' interval ends shall be changed and the ball thrown in from the centre in the first of the extra chukkers.

(NOTE.—Committees are advised to put in the sockets to hold the goal posts at the 4-yard extensions before the tournament begins.)

Prolongation in Case of Penalty.
(j) In the event of a penalty being awarded to a team that is behind in score within 20 seconds of the end of the match, the Timekeeper shall allow 20 seconds play from the time the ball is hit, or hit at, in carrying out the penalty, before he rings the final (7 minute) bell. If a goal is scored after the ball has been put into play, the final bell shall be rung,

H. P. A. GENERAL & FIELD RULES

if the original regular time (7 minutes) has expired. The match shall terminate as usual on the first stroke of the final (7 minute) bell.

(*k*) Once a match has started it shall be played to a finish unless stopped by the Umpire for some unavoidable cause, which prevents a finish the same day, such as darkness or the weather, in which case it shall be resumed at the point at which it has stopped, as to score, period and position of the ball, at the earliest convenient time, to be decided upon by the Committee conducting the tournament. **Unfinished Match.**

8.—The side that scores most goals wins the game. **How Game is Won.**

9.—No one shall be allowed to play unless he wears a protective polo helmet or polo cap, either of which must be worn with a chin strap. **Polo Helmet or Cap.**

10.—If in the opinion of the Tournament Committee the colours of two competing teams are so alike as to lead to confusion, the team lower in the draw shall be instructed to play in some other colours. **Confusing Colours.**

FIELD RULES

1.—Any infringement of the Field Rules constitutes a foul and the Umpire may stop the game. **Definition of Foul.**

2.—The Umpire shall carry a whistle, which he shall blow when he wishes to stop the game. When he does so the ball is dead until he says 'Play', and the time it is dead and not counted in the playing time of the period, except as legislated for in General Rule 7 (*f*). **Dead Ball.**

(NOTE.—If a whistle is blown for a foul at approximately the same time as a goal is scored:
  (i) The goal will be disallowed if the foul was against the attacking side and the foul is confirmed.
  (ii) The goal will be allowed if the foul was against the attacking side and the foul is over-ruled; or if the foul was against the defending side whether or not the foul is confirmed.)

3.—A pony blind of an eye may not be played; a pony showing vice, or not under proper control, shall not be allowed in the game. **Disqualified Ponies.**

4.—(*a*) Protection of Ponies by boots or bandages on all four legs is compulsory. **Equipment for Ponies.**

(*b*) Blinkers are not allowed, nor any form of noseband which obstructs the vision.

(*c*) Rimmed shoes are allowed, but the rim may only be on the inside of the shoe.

(*d*) Frost nails and screws are not allowed, but a calkin, fixed or movable is permissible, provided this is placed only at the heels of the hind shoes. The fixed or movable calkin shall be limited in size to a half inch cube.

(NOTE.—The movable calkin is allowed so that when it becomes worn it can be replaced by a fresh one without re-shoeing. The essence of this permission is that the movable calkin should resemble, as far as possible, the recognised form of fixed calkin, and it does not permit the fixing of any fancy shaped spike, nor the placing of the calkin anywhere except at the heels of the hind shoes.)

5.—(*a*) Sharp spurs are not allowed. **Disqualified Equipment for Players.**
(*b*) No player may wear buckles or studs on the upper part of his

APPENDIX III

polo boots or knee pads in such a way as could damage another player's boots or breeches.

Safety Zone.

6.—(*a*) No person is allowed on the ground during play for any purpose whatever except the players and the Umpires. A player requiring a stick, pony or other assistance from an outside person must ride to the boards, side or back lines, to procure it. No person may come on to the ground to assist him.

(*b*) No person is allowed within the Safety Zone during play except Players, Umpires, Referee, Goal Judges, Manager and Stickholders.

(NOTE.—The Safety zone is an area including the field of play, the ground within about 10 yards of the boards and the ground within about 30 yards of the goal line.)

Start of Game.

7.—At the beginning of the game the two teams shall line up in the middle of the ground, each team being on its own side of the half-way line. The Umpire shall bowl the ball underhand and hard between the opposing ranks of players, from a distance of not less than five yards, the players remaining stationary until the ball has left his hand.

How Goal is Scored.

8.—A goal is scored when a ball passes between the goal posts and over and clear of the goal line. If a ball is hit above the top of the goal posts, but in the opinion of the Umpire between those posts produced, it shall count as a goal.

Changing of Ends.

9.—(*a*) Ends shall be changed every goal except where a goal is awarded under Penalty 1. Ends shall also be changed if no goals have been hit by half-time (in a seven or five period match, after the fourth or third period respectively), and play shall be re-started at a position corresponding to the change of ends. After a goal has been hit, the game shall be re-started from the middle of the ground as prescribed by Field Rule 7. The players shall be allowed a reasonable time in which to reach the middle of the ground at a slow trot and take up their positions.

Wrong Line-up.

(*b*) If the Umpire inadvertently permits lining up the wrong way the responsibility rests with him, and there is no redress; but if at the end of the period no goal has been scored the ends shall then be changed.

Attackers Hit Behind.

10.—(*a*) The ball must go over and be clear of the back line to be out.

(*b*) When the ball is hit behind the back line by the attacking side, it shall be hit in by the defenders from the spot where it crossed the line, but at least four yards from the goal posts or boards, when the Umpire says 'play'. None of the attacking side shall be within 30 yards of the back line until the ball is hit or hit at; the defenders being free to place themselves where they choose.

Unnecessary Delay.

(*c*) The defenders shall give the attacking side reasonable time to get into position, but there shall be no unnecessary delay in hitting in. In the event of unnecessary delay the Umpires shall call on the offending side to hit in at once. If the Umpire's request is not complied with, he shall bowl in the ball underhand and hard, at the spot where the ball crossed the back line and at right angles to it.

Defenders Hit Behind.

11.—If the ball be hit behind the back line by one of the defending side, either directly or after glancing off his own pony, or after glancing off the side boards, Penalty 6 shall be exacted. If the ball strikes any other player or his pony before going behind, it shall be hit in in accordance with Field Rule 10.

H. P. A. HURLINGHAM FIELD RULES

12.—(a) The ball must go over and clear the side lines or boards **Ball Hit Out.**
to be out.

(b) When the ball is hit over the boards or side line, it must be bowled, underhand and hard, by the Umpire into the ground from a point just inside the boards or lines where it went out, on an imaginary line parallel to the two goal lines, and between the opposing ranks of players, each side being on its own side of the imaginary line. No player may stand within 10 yards of the side lines or boards. Players must remain stationary until the ball has left the Umpire's hand. A reasonable time must be allowed players in which to line up.

13.—On play being resumed after an interval, the ball shall be put **Restarting after** in play in the normal manner which would have been followed had there **Interval.** been no interval, i.e. in accordance with Field Rules 9, 10, 12, or 25, as the case may be. If the ball hits the side boards without going over them at the end of the previous period, it shall be treated as though it had been hit over them as laid down in Field Rule 12. The Umpire must not wait for players who are late.

(NOTE.—General Rule 7 (e) deals with resuming play when a period ends with a foul.)

14.—If the ball be damaged or trodden into the ground, the Umpire **Damaged Ball.** shall, at his discretion, stop the game and re-start it with a new ball, in the manner prescribed in Field Rule 25.

(NOTE.—It is desirable that the game shall be stopped and the ball changed when the damaged ball is in such a position that neither side is favoured thereby.)

15.—A player may not catch, kick or hit the ball with anything **Carrying** but his stick. He may block with any part of his body but not with an **the Ball.** open hand. He may not carry the ball intentionally. If the ball becomes lodged against a player, his pony or its equipment, in such a way that it cannot be dropped immediately, the Umpire shall blow his whistle and re-start the game in accordance with Field Rule 25 at the point where it was first carried.

16.—(a) The Right of Way: **Crossing.**

    (i) At each moment of the game there shall exist a Right of Way, which shall be considered to extend ahead of the player entitled to it, and in the direction in which he is riding.

        No player shall enter or cross this Right of Way except at such a distance that not the slightest risk of a collision or danger to either player is involved. (See *Appendix, Example II.*)

    (ii) The Right of Way, which is defined in paras. (c) to (e) below, is not to be confused with the line of the ball and does not depend on who last hit it.

(b) The Line of the Ball:

    (i) The line of the ball is the line of its course or that line produced at any moment.

    (ii) If the line of the ball changes unexpectedly, for example when a ball glances off a pony, and as a result the Right of Way changes, the player who had the Right of Way must be given room to continue a short distance on his original Right of Way.

APPENDIX III

    (iii) When a dead ball has been put into play through being hit at and missed the line of the ball is considered to be the direction in which the player was riding when he hit at it.

    (iv) If the ball becomes stationary while remaining in play, the line of the ball is that line upon which it was travelling before stopping.

(c) Player riding in direction ball is travelling:

    (i) A player following the ball on its exact line and taking it on his offside, is entitled to the Right of Way over all other players. (*See Appendix, Example II.*)

    (ii) Where no player is riding on the exact line of the ball, the Right of Way belongs to the player following it on the smallest angle, provided he does not contravene Clause (*f*). (*See Appendix, Example V.*)

    (iii) Two players when following the exact line of the ball attempting to ride one another off, share the Right of Way over all other players. (*See Appendix, Example IV.*)

    (iv) A player riding in the direction the ball is travelling at an angle to its line, has the Right of Way over a player riding to meet the ball at an angle to its line, irrespective of the width of the angle provided he does not contravene Clause (*f*). (*See Appendix, Example I.*)

    (v) No player shall be deemed to have the Right of Way by reason of his being the last striker if he shall have deviated from pursuing the exact line of the ball. (*See Appendix, Example VI.*)

(d) Equal Angles. In the rare case of two players riding in the general direction of the ball at exactly equal angles to it on opposite sides of its line, the Right of Way belongs to that player who has the line of the ball on his offside. The same rules applies as between players meeting the ball at exactly equal angles from opposite sides of its line.

(e) Player meeting the ball:

    (i) A player who rides to meet the ball on its exact line has the Right of Way over all players riding at an angle from any direction. (*See Appendix, Example III.*)

    (ii) As between players riding to meet the ball, that player has the Right of Way whose course is at the least angle to the line of the ball.

(f) Player to take ball on offside. The Right of Way entitles a player to take the ball on the offside of his pony. If he places himself to hit it on the near side and thereby in any way endangers another player who would otherwise have been clear, he loses the Right of Way and must give way to this other player. (*See Appendix, Example I.*)

(g) When two players are riding from exactly opposite directions to hit the ball each shall take it on the offside of his pony. If a collision appears probable the player who has the Right of Way must be given way to. (*See Appendix, Example I and II.*)

(h) Checking:

    (i) No player may check or pull up either on or across the Right of Way if by so doing he runs the slightest risk of collision with the player entitled to it.

H. P. A. FIELD RULES

(ii) If a player enters safely on the Right of Way and does not check, a player must not ride into him from behind, but must take the ball on the nearside of his own pony.

17.—A player may ride off an opponent, but he may not ride dangerously, as for example: **Dangerous Riding.**

(a) Bumping at an angle dangerous to a player, or his pony.

(b) Zigzagging in front of another player riding at a gallop, in such a way as to cause the latter to check his pace or risk a fall.

(c) Pulling across or over a pony's legs in such a manner as to risk tripping the pony, etc.

(d) Riding an opponent across the Right of Way. (*See Appendix, Example VII.*)

(e) Riding at an opponent in such a manner as to intimidate and cause him to pull out, or miss his stroke, although no foul or cross actually occurs.

(f) 'Sandwiching', i.e. two players of the same team riding off an opponent at the same time.

18.—No player shall seize with the hand, strike, or push with the head, hand, forearm or elbow, but a player may push with his arm, above the elbow, provided the elbow be kept close to the side. **Rough Handling.**

19.—(a) No player may hook an opponent's stick, unless he is on the same side of the opponent's pony as the ball, or in a direct line behind, and his stick is neither over or under the body or across the legs of an opponent's pony, nor may he hook or strike an opponent's stick above shoulder. The stick may not be hooked or struck level unless the opponent is in the act of striking at the ball. **Misuse of Stick.**

(b) No player may reach immediately over and across or under and across any part of an opponent's pony to strike at the ball, nor may he hit into or amongst the legs of an opponent's pony, but if a player rides from behind into the backhander of the player who has the Right of Way, he does so at his own risk and there is no foul.

(c) No player may intentionally strike his pony with his polo stick.

(d) No player may use his stick dangerously, or hold it in such a way as to interfere with another player or his pony.

20.—If a player loses his headgear the Umpire shall stop the game to enable him to recover it, but not until an opportunity occurs that neither side is favoured thereby. **Loss of Headgear.**

21.—No dismounted player may hit the ball or interfere in the game. **Dismounted Player.**

22.—(a) If a pony falls or goes lame, or if a player or pony be injured, or in the case of an accident to a pony's gear which in the opinion of the Umpire involves danger to the players or other players, the Umpire shall stop the game. **Accident or Injury.**

(b) If a player falls off his pony, the Umpire shall not stop the game, unless he is of the opinion that the player is injured. What constitutes a fall is left to the decision of the Umpire.

(c) When the game has been stopped in accordance with Clause (a) above, the Umpire shall re-start the game in the manner laid down in Field Rule 25, directly the player concerned is ready to resume play. The Umpire shall not wait for any other player who may not be present.

APPENDIX III

(d) If a player be injured, a period not exceeding 15 minutes shall be allowed for his recovery. If the injured player is unfit to play after 15 minutes, the game shall be re-started with a substitute in place of the injured player, unless Penalty 8 has been exacted. If, however, the injured player subsequently recovers he may replace the player who was substituted in his place, but the handicap of the higher handicapped player will be counted in accordance with General Rule 4 (c).

Disablement.

23.—If a player be disabled by a foul so that he is unable to continue, Penalty 8 may be exacted, or the side which has been fouled shall have the option of providing a substitute. Penalty 1, 2 or 3 shall be exacted in any case.

When Game is Not Stopped.

24.—It shall be within the discretion of the Umpire not to stop the game for the purpose of inflicting a penalty, if the stopping of the game and the infliction of the penalty would be a disadvantage to the fouled side.

Restarting When Ball was Not Out.

25.—If for any reason the game has to be stopped without the ball going out of play, it shall be re-started in the following manner. The Umpire shall stand at the spot where the ball was when the incident occurred, and facing the nearer side of the ground, but not nearer the boards or side lines than 20 yards. Both teams shall take up their positions, each team being on its own side of an imaginary line, parallel to the goal lines and extending through the Umpire to the sides of the ground. No player may stand within five yards of the Umpire. The Umpire shall bowl the ball, underhand and hard, between the opposing ranks of players, towards the nearer side of the ground, the players remaining stationary until the ball has left his hand.

Discretion of Umpires.

26.—(a) Should any incident or question not provided for in the Rules of Polo, or the Supplementary Rules of the Polo Association concerned, arise in a match, such incident or question shall be decided by the Umpire or Umpires. If the Umpires disagree, the Referee's decision shall be final.

(b) There are degrees of dangerous play and unfair play which give the advantage to the side fouling. The Penalty to be inflicted is left to the discretion of the Umpire or Umpires and shall only be referred to the Referee in the event of the Umpires disagreeing on the penalty.

PENALTIES

(NOTE.—In all free hits the ball shall be considered in play the moment it has been either hit or hit at and missed.)

Penalty Goal.
Field Rules 16, 17, 18, 19, 23.

1.—(a) If, in the opinion of the Umpire, a player commits a dangerous or deliberate foul in the vicinity of goal in order to save a goal, the side fouled shall be allowed one goal.

(b) The game shall be re-started at a spot ten yards from the middle of the fouler's goal in the manner prescribed in Field Rule 25. End shall not be changed.

30-Yard Hit.
Field Rules 16, 17, 18, 19, 23.

2.—(a) A free hit at the ball from a spot 30 yards from the goal line of the side fouling opposite the middle of the goal or, if preferred, from where the foul occurred (the choice to rest with the Captain of the side fouled); all the side fouling to be behind their back line until the ball is hit or hit at, but not between the goal posts, nor when the ball is brought into play may any of the side ride out from between the goal posts; none of the side fouled to be nearer the goal line or back line than

H. P. A. PENALTIES

the ball is, at the moment it is hit, or hit at. In the event of the Captain of the side fouled electing to take the penalty from the spot where the foul occurred none of the defending side to be within 30 yards of the ball, nor come out from between the goal posts.

(b) In carrying out Penalty 2, if the free hit would, in the opinion of the Umpire, have resulted in a goal, but is stopped by one of the side fouling coming out from between the goal posts, or crossing the back line before the ball was struck, such shot is to count as a goal to the side fouled. If the player who stopped the ball did not infringe these rules, but another member of the side did, Penalty 7 (a) shall be exacted.

3.—(a) A free hit at the ball from a spot 40 yards from the goal line of the side fouling opposite the middle of goal; all the side fouling to be behind their back line until the ball is hit or hit at, but not between the goal posts, nor when the ball is brought into play may any of the side ride out from between the goal posts; none of the side fouled to be nearer the goal line or back line than the ball is at the moment it is hit or hit at. **40-Yard Hit.** *Field Rules 16, 17, 18, 19, 23.*

(b) In carrying out Penalty 3, if the free hit would, in the opinion of the Umpire, have resulted in a goal, but is stopped by one of the side fouling coming out from between the goal posts, or crossing the back line before the ball was struck, such shot is to count as a goal to the side fouled. If the player who stopped the ball did not infringe these rules, but another member of his side did, Penalty 7 (a) shall be exacted.

4.—A free hit at the ball from a spot 60 yards from the goal line of the side fouling opposite the middle of goal, none of the side fouling to be within 30 yards of the ball, the side fouled being free to place themselves where they choose. **60-Yard Hit (Opposite Goal).** *Field Rules 16, 17, 18, 19, 21.*

5.—(a) A free hit at the ball from where it was when the foul took place, but not nearer the boards or side lines than four yards. None of the side fouling to be within 30 yards of the ball, the side fouled being free to place themselves where they choose. **Free Hit from the Spot.** *Field Rules 6, 15, 16, 17, 18, 19, 21.*

(b) A free hit at the ball from the centre of the ground, none of the side fouling to be within 30 yards of the ball, the side fouled being free to place themselves where they choose. **Free Hit from the Centre.**

6.—A free hit at the ball from a spot 60 yards distant from the back line, opposite where the ball crossed it, but not nearer the boards or side lines than four yards. None of the side fouling to be within 30 yards of the ball; the side fouled being free to place themselves where they choose. **60-Yard Hit (Opposite Where Ball Crossed).** *Field Rule 11.*

7.—(a) If the side fouling fail to carry out Penalty 2, 3, 4, 5 or 6 correctly the side fouled shall be allowed another free hit at the ball, unless a goal has been scored or awarded. If both sides fail to carry out Penalty 2 or 3 correctly, another Free Hit must be taken by the side fouled, irrespective of the result of the previous Free Hit. **Another Hit.** *Penalty 2, 3, 4, 5 or 6.*

(b) If the side fouled fail to carry out Penalty 2 or 3 correctly, the defenders shall be allowed a hit in from the middle of their own goal. None of the attacking side shall be within 30 yards of the back line until the ball is hit, or hit at; the defenders being free to place themselves where they choose. **Hit in by Defenders.** *Penalty 2 or 3.*

(c) If the attacking side fail to carry out Field Rule 10 correctly the defenders shall be allowed to hit in from the 30-yard line, from the spot opposite where the first hit was made or would have been made. None of the attackers shall be within 30 yards of the ball until it is hit or hit at; the defenders being free to place themselves where they choose. **Hit in from 30-Yard Line.** *Field Rule 10. Penalty 7 (b).*

APPENDIX III

For infringement of Penalty 7 (*b*) or any further infringement of Penalty 7 (*c*) by the attacking side, the defenders shall be allowed another hit in from the 30-yard line.

Unnecessary Delay.

(*d*) In the event of unnecessary delay by the side fouled when called on by the Umpire to take a penalty hit, the Umpire shall restart the game from the spot where the hit should have been taken in accordance with Field Rule 25.

Player to Retire.
Field Rule 23.

8.—Designation by the Captain of the side fouled of the player on the side fouling whose handicap is nearest above that of the disabled player, who shall retire from the game. If the handicap of the disabled player is higher than that of any of his opponents the player whose handicap is nearest below that of the disabled player may be designated. If there are two or more such players the Captain of the side fouled shall designate the one to retire. The game shall be continued with three players on each side, and if the side fouling refuses to continue the game, it shall thereby forfeit the match. This penalty does not apply to international matches.

Pony Disqualified.
Field Rule 3.

9.—(*a*) For infringement of Field Rule 3; the pony ordered off the ground by the Umpire and disqualified from being played again during the game or match.

(NOTE.—The case of a pony blind of an eye must be reported by the Umpire in writing to the Committee conducting the tournament who shall take all steps necessary to ensure that it shall not be played again in any tournament.)

Pony Ordered Off.
Field Rule 4.

(*b*) For infringement of Field Rule 4; the pony ordered off the ground by the Umpire and disqualified from playing again until the offence has been removed.

Player Ordered Off.
Field Rule 5.

(*c*) For infringement of Field Rule 5; the player ordered off the ground by the Umpire and disqualified from playing again until he has removed the offence.

(GENERAL NOTE.—In all the above three cases play must be restarted immediately as prescribed in Field Rule 25 and the game shall continue while the player is changing his pony or removing the offence.)

Player Excluded.

10.—The Umpire may exclude a player from the game, in addition to any other penalty, in the case of a deliberate, dangerous foul, or conduct prejudicial to the game. The side to which the excluded player belonged shall continue with three players only, or forfeit the match.

(NOTE.—The circumstances which caused this penalty to be inflicted must be reported by the Umpire in writing to the Committee conducting the tournament, to enable them to judge whether the case should be reported to higher authority.)

H. P. A. EXAMPLES

EXAMPLES OF FIELD RULES
EXAMPLE I

Field Rule 16 (*f*)　　—Loss of Right of Way.
Field Rule 16 (*g*)　　—Players riding from opposite directions must take the ball on their off-side.
Field Rule 16 (*c*) (iv)—Player riding in general direction ball is travelling entitled to Right of Way.

The ball has been hit from *X* and is about to stop at *X'*. *A* is riding in the general direction in which the ball is travelling, and provided he rides to take the ball on his off-side (which will necessitate his swerving to the left of the course he is shown as following) he will be entitled to the Right of Way shown. In this case *B* can meet the ball safely at *X'*, as both *A* and *B* will be taking the ball on their off-side. Alternatively, a player at *C* could hook *A*'s stick in safety.

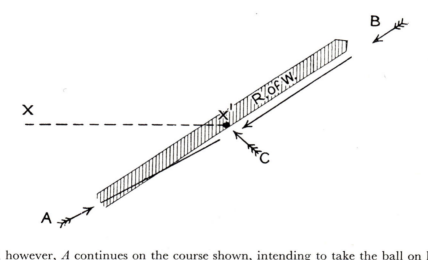

If, however, *A* continues on the course shown, intending to take the ball on his near side, he will endanger *B* or *C* and will therefore lose his Right of Way and so must keep clear of *B* or *C* as the case may be.

APPENDIX III

EXAMPLE II

Field Rule 16 (*c*) (i) —Line Follower entitled to Right of Way.
Field Rule 16 (*a*) (i) —Keeping clear of Right of Way.

A hits the ball to *X*, and follows its line to take it on his off-side. This entitles him to the Right of Way, as shown.

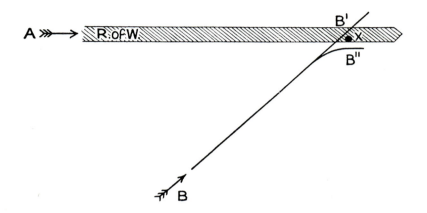

If *B* can unquestionably reach the ball at *X*, without interfering with *A*'s stroke or causing him to check in the slightest degree to avoid the risk of a collision, then the Right of Way passes to *B* and he may take an off-side backhander at *B'*.

But if there is the slightest doubt about *B* riding clear of *A*, then *A*'s Right of Way holds good and *B*'s only chance of hitting the ball is to swerve towards *B"*, keeping clear of the Right of Way, and take a near-side backhander. If in taking this backhander, or afterwards, his pony in the slightest degree enters the Right of Way, he infringes Field Rule 16 (*a*) (i).

H. P. A. EXAMPLES

EXAMPLE III

Field Rule 16 (*e*) (i) —Player meeting ball on its exact line entitled to Right of Way.
Field Rule 16 (*g*)   —Players riding from opposite directions must take the ball on their off-side.

A hits the ball in from behind to *X*.
B rides to meet it and *C* to take it on.
A collision is imminent between *B* and *C* at *X*.

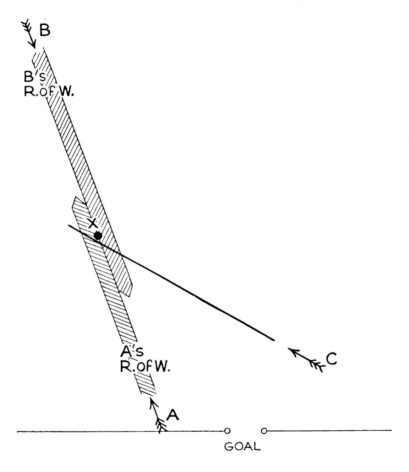

B is entitled to the Right of Way because he is meeting the ball on its exact line to take it on his off-side.

C must not cross this Right of Way.

The only way for the side hitting in to take the ball on, is for *A* to follow its line and take an off-side shot, because *A* and *B* are each entitled to their own Rights of Way, which are clear of one another.

APPENDIX III

EXAMPLE IV

Field Rule 16 (*c*) (iii)—Two players following line of ball.

The ball has been hit from the mouth of goal to *X*.

The Back (Red) and No. 1 (Blue) are following up the line of the ball, riding each other off.

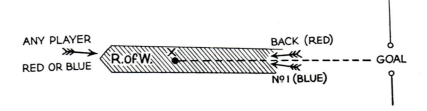

These two players share the Right of Way, as shown, and no other player, or players (Red or Blue) may cross or enter this Right of Way, even if meeting the ball on its exact line.

H. P. A. EXAMPLES

EXAMPLE V

Field Rule 16 (*c*) (ii)—Player following at Smallest Angle.
The ball has been hit to *X*.

Neither *A* nor *B* hit it there, but the striker is not near enough to the ball to risk a collision with either.

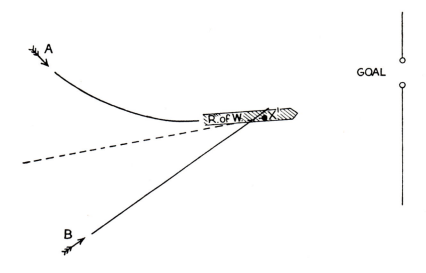

Both start to ride to the ball with equal rights.
A collision appears probable at *X*.
A has the Right of Way, as shown as he followed more closely the line on which the ball has been travelling.

APPENDIX III

EXAMPLE VI

Field Rule 16 (*c*) (v) Right of Way not dependent on who last hit the ball.
Line Follower entitled to Right of Way.

B hits the ball under his pony's neck to *X*, and swings round in a semi-circle to *B'*.
A follows the line of the ball to *A'*.
At *A' B'* a collision is imminent.

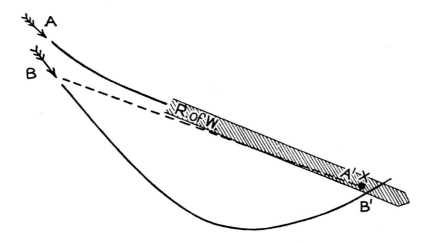

Although *B* hit the ball last he has failed to obtain the Right of Way because he has failed to follow the ball on its exact new line without deviation, whereas *A* has ridden on a line closer and more nearly parallel to the new line of the ball.

A is therefore entitled to the Right of Way.

H. P. A. EXAMPLES

EXAMPLE VII

Field Rule 17 (*d*) —Riding an opponent across the Right of Way.

No. 2 (Red) hits the ball to *X* and follows its line to take it again on his off-side. He is therefore entitled to the Right of Way, as shown.

The Back (Blue) rides for the ball. The No. 1 (Red) goes with him riding him off all the way.

A collision appears probable at *X*.

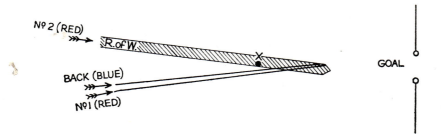

No. 1 (Red) will commit a dangerous foul if he fails to give way and consequently:
(*a*) forces the Back (Blue) across the Right of Way, thereby causing his own No. 2 (Red) to check to avoid a collision, or
(*b*) causes the Back (Blue) to check in order to avoid being sandwiched between the two Red players.

(NOTE.—In case (*a*) the Umpire must observe closely whether the Back (Blue) fouls by riding across the Right of Way of his own free will or whether the No. 1 (Red) fouls by forcing him across it.

APPENDIX IV
HURLINGHAM POLO ASSOCIATION NOTES ON THE RULES

THE REFEREE

Referee.

General Rule 5 (*a*), states: The rules shall be administered in a match, by two Umpires, who shall be mounted to enable them to keep close to the play, and a Referee who shall remain off the field of play in a central position. By mutual agreement between Captains of teams, one Umpire and, if desired, also the Referee, may be dispensed with. The decision of the Umpire shall be final, except where there are two, and they disagree, in which case the decision of the Referee shall be final.

The task of the Referee is a very responsible one, and requires continual concentration throughout the game. In many matches he may never be asked for a decision; and then, suddenly, an occasion arises when the Umpires disagree and come to the Referee for a ruling, and a definite and final opinion must be given. The Referee should, therefore, have had considerable experience of good polo, and, if possible, of umpiring. He should not only know the Rules well, but be able to refer to any Rule quickly. He should always have the Book of Rules beside him.

When the Umpires appeal to him to decide whether a foul occurred or not, the Referee should confine his decision to this point, as laid down in Field Rule 26 (*b*) and make no attempt to allocate a penalty. The reason for this is that official Umpires have a certain scale of Penalties, and once the Referee has decided whether a foul occurred, they know what Penalty to inflict. The Referee is unlikely to know the Umpire's scale, and should, therefore, refrain from allocating a Penalty unless specifically asked to do so.

The Referee should sit in a central position, at the side of the ground, *apart from distracting influences*, from which position he can see clearly and be easily accessible to the Umpires, who should know his exact position before play begins.

The Rules allow for a Referee when there is only one Umpire. In this case the Referee's duties are quite different; instead of arbitrating in case of disagreement between the Umpires he now has to act as a second Umpire to whom the mounted Umpire can appeal for assistance to decide cases in which he may not be able to see sufficiently clearly the degree of danger in a foul, etc.

THE UMPIRES

Ponies.

1.—Official and voluntary Umpires in every class of Polo must be adequately mounted. They should be sufficiently well mounted to enable them to keep close to the game without having to think of riding their ponies. The practice of Umpiring on young ponies in order to school them is strongly deprecated.

Umpires' Duties Before Game Begins

2.—(*a*) It is important that at advertised games at Polo Clubs, where public money is being taken, the game should start at the time advertised. Whilst this is really the business of the Polo Manager in a big Club, Umpires should be ready strictly on time and should ride out to the centre of the ground two minutes before the game is due to start.

(b) The Umpires should check the following points before throwing the ball in:
- (i) Who the Referee is and where he is sitting.
- (ii) That the timekeeper and Goal Judges are in position.
- (iii) In handicap matches, that the handicap is correctly put up and that both sides are satisfied with it, General Rule 7 (b).
- (iv) That they both, as well as the timekeeper, fully understand General Rule 7 (f).
- (v) That one of the Umpires should be prepared to toss for choice of goals on the arrival of the teams.

3.—(a) Before going on the ground Umpires should mutually agree to take a side line and a back line each. It is suggested that they should change sides at half time or by matches, as, if a polo ground is correctly laid out, it means that one Umpire is facing the sun the whole afternoon. **Positions. Division of Ground.**

While it is obvious that one Umpire must be responsible for throwing in from one side line or the other, it must be clearly understood that the responsibility for blowing the whistle for an infringement of the Rules in any portion of the ground is co-equal.

An Umpire on one side of the ground must not hesitate to blow his whistle if he sees a Rule being broken towards the other side of the ground, even in the near vicinity of the other Umpire, for that other Umpire may at the moment be unsighted by having ponies between him and the foul, or he may unavoidably miss it through being in the act of turning.

(b) It is essential also that one Umpire should be behind the backline when the ball is hit from behind. If an Umpire is standing behind a player hitting in from behind he will see the exact line of the ball in whatever direction it is being hit and will get a very clear view of any opposing player coming to meet the hit-in. **Hit-In.**

This meeting of the hit-in forms one of the most frequent causes of crossing, and it is important that the exact line of the ball should be observed; the other Umpire should be keeping his eye on the 30-yard line to see that the opponents of the side hitting in do not cross the line before the ball is hit or hit at.

(c) It is even more essential that one Umpire should be on the goal line in 30 and 40 yard hits as the defending side may not cross the back line until the ball is hit or hit at, or come out between the goal posts. Infringement of this Rule has such strong Penalties that it is obvious that an Umpire should be on the goal line, otherwise it will be impossible to detect this infringement. *Penalties 2 and 3.*

(d) In the case of the 60 yard hits and the free hits (in the event of the later being fairly near goal) it is also important that an Umpire should be close behind the line in the melees which frequently result from those Penalties close in front of goal, the hooking of sticks on the wrong side often occurs, and the defenders may hit behind and it is difficult to see unless the Umpire is close. *Penalties 4 and 5 (a) and (b).*

(e) It follows that if these positions are mutually agreed to by the two Umpires, the general position of the two Umpires, whatever direction the game goes in, will be that one Umpire will be more or less at a short distance behind the game while the other is galloping level with it.

APPENDIX IV

It is considered that this is the ideal combination of the two positions to make certain of seeing every possible infringement of the Rules.

Use of Whistle.
General Rule 7 (f).

4.—(a) Be careful to use the whistle correctly. Remember there is a timekeeper who has to stop the clock when you blow one firm blast, but who must not stop the clock when you blow two sharp blasts. Read General Rule 7 (f) carefully and note the occasions when to blow one firm blast and when to blow two sharp ones. In both cases the ball is dead until you say 'Play' (Field Rule 2), but in the latter case the time it is dead counts in the playing time of the period and in the former it does not: you must be very careful to blow the whistle in the correct manner. Although you should not normally blow the whistle when the attacking side hit behind you must be on the lookout to do so if the defending side hit behind, as this will entitle the attackers to a 60-yard hit opposite where the ball crossed.

(b) The Umpire should carry his whistle in his hand ready for instant use and must make up his mind in a flash and blow without hesitation. Owing to the pace at which polo is played, any momentary delay is fatal, as situations change so rapidly that an Umpire may end by not blowing his whistle at all for a foul that he really meant to give. A small stick with a whistle fitted at one end is recommended.

(c) The Umpire having blown his whistle should quickly check with the other Umpire that he agrees there was a foul and to the proposed penalty, this can be done either verbally or preferably by a nod of the head or some other prearranged signal, it is most important that there should be no delay through long discussion.

The Umpire should then loudly and clearly announce the foul and penalty, thus 'Cross against Red, Free hit from the spot', and without waiting canter to the spot where the foul occurred, drop the ball and go to his position. There is no necessity to state the number of the penalty awarded.

Referee.

5.—If the Umpires disagree they should refer the matter to the Referee to final decision; but they should confine their first request to a decision as to whether or not a foul occurred and only ask for a decision as to the Penalty if they are unable to agree on this point also. The reason for this is that the official Umpires have a certain scale of penalties and, once the Referee has decided whether a foul occurred, they know what penalties to inflict. The Referee is unlikely to know the Umpires' scale and should therefore refrain from allocating a Penalty unless specially asked to do so.

Two good Umpires will only rarely need to consult the Referee, but if there is only one Umpire, he should use the Referee as a second Umpire to whom he can appeal for assistance to decide cases in which he may not be able to see sufficiently clearly the degree of danger in the foul.

Concentration.

6.—Owing to the speed at which it is played, polo is the most difficult of all games to Umpire. The Umpire must be concentrated on the play every moment of the period; he should be watching the game so closely that he is certain of the line of the ball each time it has been hit, and, consequently, knows at a glance which Player has the Right of Way. He must further establish the direction of the Right of Way (in his mind) bearing in mind that it is very likely that the Right of Way and the line of the ball will not coincide. The moment the line of the ball is changed he must quickly know who is now entitled to the Right of Way and in what direction the new Right of Way lies. Attention is drawn to Field Rule 16 (b) (ii). It is the Umpire's job to see that the player who has Right of Way is given sufficient room to pull up or turn when the Right of Way changes suddenly.

A common error among inexperienced Umpires is lack of concentration due to watching some brilliant individual or combined play, more from an appreciation of the Players' point of view than as an Umpire.

7.—Captains shall have the sole right to discuss with the Umpire or Umpires any matter arising during the game: but no player shall appeal in any manner to the Umpire for fouls. This includes a player holding up his stick, for which he may be penalised after a warning under Field Rule 26. If thought necessary a general caution to all players should be given at the beginning of a match or chukker, after which any appeal for a foul may be penalised without further warning. *No Appealing. General Rule 5 (d).*

It is very necessary that there should be no hanging about or long discussions between Umpires, and the right of a Captain or a side to discuss matters with the Umpire does not include the right to challenge the Umpire's normal decisions.

Never get into an argument with the Players. It is unnecessary to discuss anything with the Players while playing; or explain reasons for giving any decisions; but, in the interests of the game, when it is finished a discussion of the game and the fouls that occurred will be found helpful, especially to young players.

8.—Remember that if the game ends in a tie at the end of the final period the game must carry on after the bell is rung until the ball goes out of play or the 30-second bell is rung. *Prolongation in the Event of a Tie. General Rule 7 (h).*

9.—Read carefully Note to Field Rule 2 as to when a goal may be allowed to stand after the whistle is blown for a foul. *Allowing a Goal after Whistle.*

10.—The method of dealing with offences under these Rules is given in detail in Penalties 9 (a), (b) and (c) respectively. These offences concern unmanageable ponies, blinkers, frost nails, sharp spurs and protruding buckles on boots and knee pads. The Umpire should ride up to the Captain of the team and direct him to tell the player to change his pony or remove the offence. *Field Rules 3, 4 and 5.*

Note that if a pony is disqualified (Penalty 9) (a) or a Player is excluded (Penalty 10) a written report is required from the Umpire.

11.—Remember that, if by half-time no goals have been scored, ends will be changed. *Changing Ends. Field Rule 9.*

Remember also, that if a goal has been scored, it is laid down that teams should return to the centre at the pace of a slow trot. It will be found that, in an exciting match, when the score is level or nearly level and the last period is being played, one team or the other, or both, will gallop back to the centre to get the ball thrown in. Remember to stick to the trot when returning to the throw-in.

12.—(a) It is difficult to lay down an exact distance as to what constitutes a cross, but in all doubtful cases the pace at which the players are moving must be considered, or whether there was any danger involved, as on this depends the question whether the Player entitled to the Right of Way has to check to avoid a collision. The benefit of the doubt should be in favour of the man entitled to the Right of Way. *Crossing. Field Rule 16.*

The good Umpire gets consistent in giving Penalties for crossing, and this is more appreciated by the players than anything else.

APPENDIX IV

(b) A frequent form of foul is committed by a Player swinging his pony across the Right of Way immediately before or after hitting at the ball. This often occurs after taking a near-side backhander. Another foul under this Rule is checking for a backhander (even when the striker is entitled to the Right of Way) when an opponent is following close behind in full pursuit. On the other hand, once a Player has safely taken over the Right of Way from another Player, the latter may not ride into the former from behind unless the former checks his pony.

(c) Umpires are apt to forget that a Player riding in the direction that the ball is travelling at an angle to its line, has the Right of Way over a Player riding to meet the ball at an angle to its line, irrespective of the width of the angle, provided he takes the ball on his off-side.

It is only when a Player rides to meet the ball on its exact line that he has the Right of Way over all other Players riding at an angle from any direction.

Dangerous Angle.
Field Rule 7 (a).

13.—The Umpire when deciding whether a bump was made at a dangerous angle, should consider the speed at which the Player was riding and whether the bump could have caused the pony to fall, for example a bump behind the saddle at an acute angle.

Players should straighten out almost parallel with their opponents before riding them off.

Intimidation.
Field Rule 17 (e).

14.—This Rule should be carefully read and strictly enforced.

Misuse of Stick.
Field Rule 19.

15.—The Rule states that the stick may be only hooked or struck when an adversary is in the act of striking at the ball and that a Player is not allowed to strike or hook an opponent's stick above the level of the shoulder.

It should be noted that no player may strike at the ball among the legs of an adversary's pony and that the hind legs are included in this Rule. However, if a Player rides into the backhander of a Player entitled to the Right of Way, he does so at his own risk.

The same Rule states that no Player shall intentionally strike his pony with his polo stick. The U.S.P.A. Rule applies only to the head of the stick, but under the H.P.A. Rule a Player is prohibited from intentionally striking his pony with the shaft or even thumping it with the butt end of the handle.

Some examples of dangerous use of stick are:

(a) Taking a full swing at the ball from the throw-in or in a scrimmage in such a way as to endanger other Players.

(b) Striking hard into a group of ponies legs during a scrimmage.

(c) Striking at the ball in the air so as to endanger other players.

(d) Taking a full swing under a pony's neck in such a way as to endanger a Player riding alongside.

(e) Striking an opponent's stick in such a way as may cause injury to an opponent.

As a general rule Umpires are not sufficiently strict about giving these fouls.

Accident or Injury.
Field Rule 22 (a).

16.—This Rule states: 'If a pony falls or goes lame, or if a player or pony be injured, or in case of an accident to a pony's gear which, in the opinion of the Umpire, involves danger to a player, or other players, the Umpire shall stop the game.'

H. P. A. NOTES ON THE RULES

For example the following can be considered:

(a) Broken Martingale, if end trails on the ground.
(b) Broken girth.
(c) Broken reins, if single.
(d) Broken headstall, allowing bit to fall out.
(e) Loose bandages or boots, if they fall off game continues.

The game is not stopped for:

(f) Broken Martingale, if *not* dangerous.
(g) Lost or broken leathers.
(h) Broken curb chain.
(i) Lost bandages or boots.
(j) Responsibility for deciding what is or not dangerous, however, must remain with the Umpire.

17.—'It shall be within the discretion of the Umpire not to stop the game for the purpose of inflicting a Penalty, if the stopping of the game and the infliction of the Penalty would be to the disadvantage of the side fouled.' **When Game is Not Stopped. Field Rule 24.**

This is one of the most difficult rules to apply, for if the Umpire refrains from blowing his whistle because he thinks the striker is bound to get a goal, it is perfectly all right if he gets the goal, but should he miss, it is both unfortunate and awkward.

18.—This Rule empowers Umpires to penalise all dangerous and unfair play and bad behaviour on the ground that is not mentioned in the Rules. **Discretion of Umpires. Field Rule 26.**

19.—(a) There are no less than five separate Penalty hits (Penalties 2 to 5 (b)): **Penalties.**

    (i) The 30-yard Hit.
    (ii) The 40-yard Hit.
    (iii) The 60-yard Hit.
    (iv) The Free Hit from the Spot.
    (v) The Free Hit from the Centre of the Ground.

As regards the actual Penalties themselves: there are eleven. Umpires must know these by heart, but there is no longer any need to know the numbers, since the Rules give the name to each Penalty, which should be used in preference to the number.

(b) The ruling of a Penalty Goal states: 'If, in the opinion of the Umpire, a Player commits a dangerous or deliberate foul in the vicinity of goal in order to save a goal, the side fouled shall be allowed one goal.' *Penalty 1.*

The Umpire, having awarded a Penalty Goal, shall immediately instruct the goal judge to wave the white flag.

When throwing in from the spot ten yards in front of the goal it is preferable that the ball should be thrown in towards the side of the ground where the foul took place.

A clear definition is sometimes asked for as to what 'vicinity' means in terms of distance from the goal.

The fact that the foul is considered to have been committed in order to save a goal obviously denotes that the Player fouled is in a position to score, and is therefore, in most cases, close to the goal. It is difficult to lay down any actual distance to cover 'vicinity', but this

APPENDIX IV

Penalty Goal has seldom been given at distances exceeding the 40-yard line unless the Player fouled is more or less in front of goal and had an open run at the goal if he had not been fouled.

Penalty 2.

(c) Remember that the wording for a 30-yard Hit is: 'A free hit at the ball from a spot 30 yards from the goal line of the side fouling, opposite the middle of the goal, or, if preferred, from where the foul occurred (the choice to rest with the Captain of the side fouled . . .)' . . . It is therefore, clear that an Umpire, if the foul occurs anywhere nearer the goal than 30 yards, should immediately ride up to the Captain of the side fouled and offer him the choice of a Free Hit from 30 yards or from the place where the foul occurred; he should not decide this matter himself, and he should remember that in the latter case the fouling side may not be within 30 yards of the ball, nor may they come out between the goal posts.

Penalty 2 and 3

(d) It is of utmost importance to remember that in carrying out 30 or 40 yard hits, if the hit would, in the opinion of the Umpires, have resulted in a goal, but is stopped by one of the side fouling coming out between the goal posts, or crossing the back line before the ball was struck, such a shot is to count as a goal to the side fouled. If the Player who stopped the ball did not infringe these Rules, but another member of the side did, then the fouled side should be allowed another hit from the same position (Penalty 7 (a)).

This bears out the importance of one Umpire being on the goal-line.

Penalty 4 and 5 (a).

(e) Remember that, in 60-yard Hits and Free Hits from the spot and centre, the Umpires should see that the side fouling should stand back 30 yards from the ball before it is hit or hit at. In view of the fact that there are a large number of 60-yard hits, Umpires can train their eyes very quickly as to what 30 yards is, as there is a 30 yard line marked on the ground as well as a 60-yard line.

Remember that a Free Hit (i.e. from where the foul took place) can be as severe as a 30 to 40-yard Hit, for it is clear that if an infringement of the Rules takes place, say, 15 yards in front of the goal for which the Umpire decides that a Free Hit is suitable, the side fouling must be 30 yards from the ball when it is hit or hit at, and will, therefore, be 15 yards behind the goal, thus making the goal almost a certainty; and if an infringement occurs calling for the exercise of a 60-yard Hit opposite goal or a Free Hit from where the foul took place, at a point nearer the goal line than 60 yards, then a Free Hit from the spot should generally be given and the side fouled get the benefit of having the better chance of hitting a goal than if they had been given Penalty 4 and taken back to 60 yards. However, the gravity of the infringement must be the deciding factor in the Umpire's decision.

Penalty 5 (b).

(f) Umpires should bear in mind that the object of Penalty 5 (b) a Free Hit from the centre of the ground, is to give Umpires an additional Penalty, which may be awarded at their discretion, in circumstances where a Free Hit from the spot is considered inadequate and to award a 60-yard Hit would be too severe.

For example: the attacking side commit a minor infringement in the vicinity of the defenders' 60-yard line. An Umpire may award a Free Hit from the centre of the ground if he considers a free Hit from the spot inadequate and a Penalty 4 too severe, as this would entail taking the attackers back behind their 60-yard line.

H. P. A. NOTES ON THE RULES
THE TIMEKEEPER

General Rule 6, page 123 states; 'An Official Timekeeper and Scorer shall be employed in all games and matches'.

The length of each period is 7 minutes.[1] The time during which a penalty is being exacted or an accident being dealt with does not count in the 7 minutes playing time. The fact that the time is not to be counted (i.e. the clock is to be stopped) is indicated by the Umpire blowing one firm blast on his whistle. The time starts to count again (i.e. the clock is to be started) when the Umpire says 'Play' and the ball is hit or hit at.

The Timekeeper will find no difficulty in excluding the time required for Penalties and accidents from the playing time of the period if he is provided with a proper polo stop-clock.

If none is available, two ordinary stop-watches will do, one being used to record the time from the commencement of the period and the other for noting the time to be added to the first watch on account of Penalties and accidents.

The Timekeeper must note that if the Umpire blows two sharp blasts the time that the ball is dead is to be included in the playing time and, therefore, no action is required by the Timekeeper.

It is the Timekeeper's duty to ring the bell when the 7 minute period finishes, and again 30 seconds later if play has not already stopped. Great care must be taken that the first stroke of the bell coincides exactly with the termination of the 7 and $7\frac{1}{2}$ minutes, for, in the case of a close match, in a final period, a ball may pass between the goal posts a second before or after the correct time of the conclusion of the period. The Timekeeper's responsibility in this matter is, therefore, of great importance.

Between each period there is an interval of 3 minutes. In all matches there is a half-time interval of 5 minutes. Should play begin before the 3 minutes are up, it is unnecessary to ring the bell but the clock should be started at the moment that play begins. If the play has not begun at the end of each interval the Timekeeper shall ring the bell, but he must not start the clock until play actually begins.

In the event of a tie requiring that an extra period be played, the interval shall be 5 minutes. In this case it is the Umpire's duty to see that the game is not started again until the 5 minutes interval has been taken.

General Rule 7 (j), page 124, is extremely important to the Timekeeper, as he is the only official who can carry out this rule. It reads: 'In the event of a penalty being awarded to a team that is behind in score within twenty seconds of the end of a match, the Timekeeper shall allow 20 seconds play from the time the ball is hit, or hit at, in carrying out the penalty, before he rings the final bell. If a goal is scored after the ball has been put into play, the final bell shall be rung, if the original regular time has expired. The match shall terminate, as usual, on the first stroke of the final bell.'

Thus, if the whistle blows for any foul committed by the team that is leading when there is less than 20 seconds to go before time in the final period, it is the clear duty of the Timekeeper to allow 20 seconds more play from the time the ball is hit, or hit at, in taking the penalty.

[1] *In the United States any overtime played in a period is deducted from the 7 minutes of the next period.*

APPENDIX IV

The Timekeeper should be provided with a white flag. When the Goal Judge signals a goal by waving his white flag, the Timekeeper should acknowledge by waving his flag in reply; he must keep the score on a proper form, and see that the score is correctly put up on the board.

The Timekeeper should fully understand Penalty 1 (Penalty Goal), page 130, when the Umpire orders the Goal Judge to signal a goal as a result of a foul in the vicinity of goal, and throws in the ball to re-start the game at a spot ten yards from the middle of the fouler's goal:[1] also General Rule 7 (*f*), (i) and (ii), page 124, correct use of whistle.

In International and important Open Cup matches, Committees are recommended to appoint a member of the Committee, or designate some suitable official, to sit with the Timekeeper to assist him in his responsible duties.

THE GOAL JUDGES

The duty of signalling goals each end is usually undertaken by a member of the ground staff, and this duty is generally efficiently carried out.

General Rule 5 (*b*), page 123, reads: 'In important matches Goal Judges shall be appointed each of whom shall give testimony to the Umpires at the latter's request in respect of goals or other points of the game near his goal, but the Umpires shall make all decisions'.

A flag should be waved, when a goal is scored, until acknowledged by the Timekeeper.

This flag should be kept down and furled until a goal is scored.

Remember, an Umpire may order a Goal Judge to signal a goal for Penalty 1 without the ball having actually passed through the goal.

When the ball is hit behind, a Goal Judge should quickly place a new ball on the spot where it crossed the line, remembering that it must not be nearer than four yards to the goal-posts or the side boards.

Remember, the Umpires may at any moment ask the Goal Judge's opinion on the question of whether the defending side hit the ball behind the goal-line or on other points of the game near the goal. They, however, make all decisions.

Sometimes the ball rolls only a few inches over the goal-line between the posts, or is hit back again by a defender just as it has crossed the line. This must be carefully watched for.

Goal Judges should wear white coats (long ones are not recommended), and keep out of the way of the players.

It is recommended that in important matches two Goal Judges should be appointed each end. They should be polo players, and energetic.

Many polo players and Umpires will remember difficult situations when a goal has been shot at from an acute angle, particularly if the ball has passed above the level of the goal posts. The normal single Goal Judge standing well back behind the centre of the goal, may be in doubt whether it was a goal, but must either signal a goal or not. The Umpire, whose decision is final, can intervene but may or may not have been in a position to see more clearly than the Goal Judge.

[1] *Under U.S.P.A. Rules a Penalty goal is followed by a 40-Yard Hit instead of a throw-in.*

H. P. A. NOTES ON THE RULES

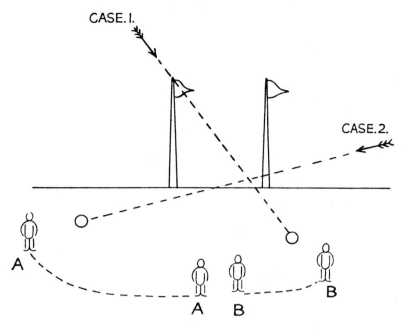

If two Goal Judges are posted each end such a situation should not occur. They can stand together behind the goal when the game is running towards the other goal; but the moment an attack on their goal is coming, one of them should always keep moving, so as to keep the approaching ball in view through the goal-posts, particularly when it is actually struck at goal.

Example:

Case 1.—The game has come down the left side of the ground, and Goal Judge 'B' moves out on the imaginary dotted line to the right, watching the approaching ball between the goal-posts. Goal Judge 'A' remains in the centre.

Case 2.—The game has come down the right side of the ground; Goal Judge 'A' moves out on the imaginary dotted line to the left, watching the approaching ball between the goal-posts. Goal Judge 'B' remains in the centre.

APPENDIX V

H. P. A. DIRECTIVE ON RULES RE SUBSTITUTION

1.—The basic rule is that no player may play for two teams in one tournament. (General Rule 4 (*e*).)

2.—Provided this point does not arise the interpretation of the rules is quite simple.

3.—In fact the only criterion is that the player must be qualified and the team must remain qualified after the substitution has been made.

4.—This applies equally to a substitute:

(*a*) who plays for a team in its first match of a tournament.

Thus e.g. If a team enters in a 20-goal tournament as a 13-goal side and if for one reason or another a 1-goal player is unable or unwilling to play there is nothing to prevent him being substituted for by an 8-goal player provided that player has not played or is not playing in any other team.

(*b*) who plays in a team after that team has played in one or more matches.

(*c*) who has to come in during the middle of a match. Again an 8-goal player could be substituted for a 1-goal player provided the team was still qualified, although in a match played on handicap, as the team would then have to give away an extra $4\frac{1}{2}$ goals (in a 4-chukker match) they would not be likely to choose such a substitute unless the substitution took place very early on during the match.

5.—So far the position is quite clear: but under the Rule tournament committees are given the discretion of allowing a player to play for more than one team under the following circumstances:

(*a*) If there is no suitable player available who has not already played. A suitable player is defined as someone with a handicap not more than 2 goals less than the player he is to replace.

(*b*) If they are satisfied that there is a *bona fide* need for a substitute.

(*c*) If the total handicap of the team requiring a substitute will not be increased thereby.

(NOTE.—Where there is only one substitute this condition is quite straightforward—the substitute's handicap must not be more than that of the player he replaces.)

Where there is more than one substitute the following is suggested:

(i) If the team has already played it should be the handicap of the team the last time it had played that should count.

(ii) No question of substitution under the Rule should be considered until a team is complete.

(*d*) If, in matches with an international flavour, the Captain of the opposing side agrees.

H. P. A. DIRECTIVE ON SUBSTITUTION

6.—The interpretation of this Rule often causes difficulties. It is not possible to mention all contingencies and tournament committees must make their own decisions, but it is thought that the following suggestions may be of help to them.

7.—It is generally agreed that the less the basic rule (para. 1) is broken the better but nonetheless there are certain circumstances where it cannot be avoided.

Such circumstances can arise under three categories:

(a) Substitution arranged before a match is due to start.

(b) Substitution at the last moment before a game starts owing to a player failing to turn up.

(c) Substitution after a match has started due to 'sickness, accident or duty'.

8.—Category A. This is the category where it is least likely for it to be justifiable for a substitute to be played who has already played in another team, and the tournament committees should be most reluctant to use their discretion.

But supposing there were a final between Team X and Team Y which are both 12-goal teams: supposing also Team Y includes a 7-goal player who becomes incapacitated and there is not anyone available, who has not already played, higher than a 2 handicap, then unless the tournament committee exercise their discretion, the final would be 12 goals against 7 goals and probably spoilt as a good match.

Nonetheless it can be argued that this would be a better solution than breaking the basic rule and allowing another 7 or even a 5-goal player who had already played to act as a substitute. A decision in such a case must be at the discretion of the tournament committee but they should certainly not allow a substitute to play who is still in the tournament.

9.—Categories B and C. The problems in both these categories are very similar viz.: where there is a need for a substitute owing either to a player turning up late or to an accident after a match has started.

It is suggested that in cases with an 'emergency' element such as this:

(a) A player who is in another team in the same tournament, whether or not he has already played, should be allowed to play as a substitute provided he is qualified under para. 5 above and he should not thereby be disqualified from continuing with his original team.

(b) If a player who had already played in one team has been allowed to play for another team because there was no suitable substitute at the time, he should be allowed to continue with that team in the next round even if there were then a suitable substitute available but only if the team for which he first played was not still in the tournament, provided the original player is still not available.

(c) If a player is late and the game is started with a substitute, the late player may replace the substitute after the first chukka but not thereafter.

10.—In the prospectus of a tournament with a subsidiary tournament it should be clearly stated whether or not the main tournament and the subsidiary count as one tournament for the purposes of the substitution rules.

APPENDIX VI
THE UNITED STATES POLO ASSOCIATION
RULES OF POLO
INDEX

GENERAL RULES

	PAGE
1. Ponies	153
2. Ground; Goals	153
3. Balls	153
4. Number of Players; Substitute Players in Matches and Tournaments	153
5. Officials, Umpire, Referee, Goal Referees	154
6. Timekeeper and Scorer	154
7. Maximum Duration of Play; Shorter Duration, Handicap Calculation; Play Continuous; Termination of Period; Determination of Time; Last Period; Prolongation in case of Tie; Prolongation in case of Penalty; Unfinished Games	154/5
8. Most Goals Win Game	156
9. Headgear	156
10. Conflicting Colours	156
11. Fines	156
12. Handicaps	156

FIELD RULES

1. Ponies	156
2. Equipment Prohibited	156
3. Shoeing Restrictions	156
4. Ground kept Clear	156
5. Infringement a Foul	156
6. Whistle, Dead Ball	156
7. How Game Commences	157
8. Ends changed; Wrong Line-Up	157
9. Goals, Over Top of Goal Posts	157
10. Ball Hit Behind by Attacking Side	157
11. Ball Hit Across Back Line	158
12. Ball Out; Ball Bowled in by Umpire	158
13. Ball Put in Play	158
14. Ball Damaged, etc.	158
15. Carrying Ball, etc.	159
16. Crossing; Right of Way; Rider to meet it; Line of the Ball	159/60
17. Dangerous Riding	160
18. Rough Play	160
19. Hooking Sticks; Striking Pony with Head of Stick	159/60
20. No Outside Assistance on Ground	161
21. Dismounted Player	161
22. Accidents	161
23. Disablement by Foul	161
24. Incidents not Provided for by Rules	161

PENALTIES

1.	162
2.	162
3.	162
4.	162
5.	163
6.	163
7.	163
8.	163
9.	163
10.	163

EXAMPLES OF FIELD RULES

I. 16 (i)	165
II. 16	166
III. 16	167
IV. 16 (b), 16 (c)	168
V. 17 (d)	169

APPENDIX VI

THE UNITED STATES POLO ASSOCIATION RULES OF POLO

GENERAL RULES

1.—Ponies of any height may be played. **Ponies.**

2.—(a) A full-sized playing field shall be 300 yards in length by 200 yards in width, if unboarded; and 300 yards in length by 160 yards in width if boarded. **Ground.**

    (i) The boundaries on the sides of the playing field shall be known as the side boards or side lines.

    (ii) The boundaries at the ends of the field shall be known as the back lines.

    (iii) The imaginary line that divides the field equally at right angles to the side lines or side boards shall be known as the centre line.

    (iv) In addition to the field of play, there shall be an area of about 10 yards from the side lines and about 30 yards from the back lines. This area shall be known as the safety zone and incidents which occur here shall be treated as though they were on the playing field.

(b) The goals shall be the centre 8 yards of each back line between two goal posts. **Goals.**

(c) The goal posts shall be at least 10 feet high, round and of equal diameter throughout. They shall be in a vertical position and light enough to break upon collision.

(d) The boards shall not exceed 11 inches in height. It is permissible to use triangular pieces of wood at the bottom of the side boards toward the playing field to deflect the ball from the side boards. These pieces shall not be over 3 inches wide nor more than 3 inches high.

3.—The ball shall be within the limits of 3 to $3\frac{1}{2}$ inches in diameter and $3\frac{1}{4}$ to $4\frac{1}{2}$ ounces in weight. **Balls.**

4.—(a) The number of players is limited to four a side in all games and matches. All players shall play the stick with the right hand, with the exception of left-handers registered with the Association prior to January 1, 1974. **Number of Players.**

(b) A player shall not play in any event on more than one team. *Penalty 9.*

(c) A player may be substituted for another during a match only if the latter player, through sickness or accident, is unable to continue. In such case, the handicap of the player having the higher handicap shall be counted. A substitution may be made during a tournament event if a member of a team is for any reason unable to finish the event, or if a member of a team has, for any reason, been unable to play during the earlier stages of the event. In all cases of substitution, the substitute must be qualified to play in the event and the team must remain qualified **Substitute Players in Matches and Tournaments.**

APPENDIX VI

for the event, after the substitution has been made. The disabled player shall replace the substitute if and when able to do so, but only after the game in which the substitution occurred has been completed.

Officials, Umpire Referee.

5.—(a) The officials for a tournament series shall be two Umpires and a Referee appointed by the Committee. In non-tournament matches, there shall be one Umpire, or two Umpires and a Referee. All decisions of the Umpire, or agreed decisions of two Umpires, shall be final. In the event two are serving and they disagree, the final decision shall be made by the Referee. Procedures laid down in these rules for 'the Umpire' shall apply to one or both Umpires as applicable.

(b) The Committee shall furnish the Umpires mounts suitable for the calibre of the game and the Referee a seat at a vision free point opposite the centre of the playing field. The Referee shall also be provided with an up-dated set of Rules and the Guide for Umpires of the U.S.P.A. The latter two shall be for the exclusive use of the Officials and Team Captains.

(c) The authority of the Umpire and/or Referee shall extend from the time each game or match is scheduled to start until its end, and it shall include recommending to the Association the suspension of a player whose conduct is not in the best interest of the sport. All questions arising at other times shall be resolved by the Committee.

(d) Captains shall have the sole right to dicuss with the Umpire or Umpires questions arising during the game. No player shall appeal in any manner to the Umpire or Umpires for fouls. This does not preclude a captain from discussing any matter with the Umpire. Any player aggrieved by the conduct or competency of the Officials or the Committee may file a complaint with the Circuit Governor, who shall make an investigation and report his findings at the next meeting of the Officers and Governors of the Association.

Goal Referees.

(e) In important matches Goal Referees should be appointed, each of whom shall give testimony to the Umpires at the latters' request to goals or other points of the game near his goal, but the Umpire shall make all decisions.

Timekeeper and Scorer, Supplies.

6.—The Committee shall provide an official Timekeeper and an official Scorer. A vantage point, free of visual obstructions toward the playing field, shall also be provided, as well as an air horn, a bell, a clock and score sheets. In addition to his duty of timing the game, the Timekeeper shall sound the air horn loudly two minutes before each period as a warning of its commencement.

Maximum Duration of Play.

7.—(a) A match shall be 6 periods of 7 minutes each with intervals of four minutes after each period, except at half time and after the last period in case of a tie when the interval shall be 10 minutes.

Shorter Duration Handicap Calculation.

(b) The conditions of a tournament may prescribe a less number of periods to constitute a match in any event. If matches under handicap conditions are played of shorter duration, the handicap shall be worked out proportionately according to the number of periods played. Fractions of a goal of one-half or more shall be counted as a goal.

Play Continuous.

(c) Except where otherwise specified in these rules, play shall be continuous; and no time shall be taken out for a change of ponies.

Termination of Period.

(d) Each period of play except the last period shall terminate, after the expiration of the 7 minutes (designated by the sounding of a horn) and as soon as the ball goes out of play or hits the boards. A bell shall be rung 30 seconds after the horn signal and the period shall terminate,

U.S.P.A. GENERAL RULES

although the ball is still in play, at the stroke of the bell, wherever the ball may be.

(NOTE.—In all cases the Umpire's whistle is the controlling factor. Players must continue to play until the whistle is blown.)

(e) If a foul is given after the horn signal the Umpire's whistle terminates the period and the penalty shall be exacted at the beginning of the next period, except as laid down hereafter in subsections (i) and (j) of this Rule.

(f) If and when, during a period, the Umpire stops the play, the time that elapses before the resumption of play shall not be deducted from the period. **Determination of Time.**

  (i) If play is to be resumed by the Umpire bowling in the ball between the teams, play does not resume until the ball leaves the Umpire's hand.
  (ii) If play is to be resumed by a team hitting in from its back line, play does not resume until the Umpire says 'Play' and the ball is hit or hit at.
  (iii) If play is to be resumed by a fouled side making a free hit at the ball it was awarded on a foul, play does not resume until the Umpire says 'Play' and the ball is hit or hit at.

(g) The last period shall terminate, although the ball is still in play, at the sound of the horn signal, wherever the ball may be, except in case of a tie. **Last Period.**

(h) In the case of a tie, after 7 minutes of play in the last period, the horn shall be sounded, but play shall continue until a goal is scored, the ball goes out of play, hits the side boards or crosses the side lines, or until the 30 second bell is sounded. Should the score still then be tied, the game shall be resumed after an interval of 10 minutes, from where the ball went out of play, in periods played under the same conditions as the one described before in this paragraph, with 4 minute intervals in between each period, until one side obtains a goal, which shall determine the match. **Prolongation in Case of Tie.**

(i) Should there be a tie in the last period and a penalty, other than Penalty No. 1, be exacted with less than 20 seconds left in the regular or extended period, 20 seconds shall be added to the period. The free hit shall be taken immediately and the period shall continue until:

  (i) The regular 7 minute period has expired and a goal has been made.
  (ii) Or, in the time frame beyond 7 minutes of the period a goal has been made, the ball goes out of play, or the added time expires.
  (iii) Or, another foul has been called.

(j) If a penalty is given in the last period in favour of a team that is behind and there is not twenty seconds of playing time left in the game, twenty seconds of time shall be allowed from the time that the ball is put into play to give the team that was fouled a chance to realise on the penalty. In case a goal is scored after the ball has been put into play, the final bell shall be rung, if the original regular time has expired. **Prolongation in Case of Penalty.**

(k) Once a match has started, it shall be played to a finish unless stopped by darkness or the weather, in which case it shall be resumed at the point at which it stopped, as to score, period and position of the ball, **Unfinished Games.**

APPENDIX VI

at the earliest convenient time, to be decided upon by the committee conducting the tournament or match.

Most Goals Win Game.

8.—The side that scores most goals wins the game. Goals awarded under Penalty No. 1 and by handicap shall count as goals scored.

Headgear.

9.—No one shall be allowed to play unless he wears a protective helmet or cap equipped with a chin strap, the chin strap to be worn during play under the chin.

Conflicting Colours.

10.—If, in the opinion of the committee conducting any tournament, the colours of two competing teams are so alike as to lead to confusion, the team lower in the draw shall be instructed to play in some other colours. The committee shall give reasonable notice of this. In match games, the team required to play in some other colours shall be determined by lot.

Fines.

11.—The Umpire shall have the power to impose a fine (the amount not to exceed $50.00, payable to the U.S.P.A.) on any team or member of a team failing to appear within a reasonable time of the starting time of a match, or for any misconduct on the field such as a disrespectful attitude toward the Umpire or other players or for a violation of the rules during the progress of a match, and shall report the same in writing to the committee in charge for enforcement.

Handicaps.

12.—Where the word 'handicaps' is used in these rules, it refers to the official handicap of the Association.

FIELD RULES

Ponies.
Penalty 9.

1.—(a) No pony shall be eligible to play on more than one team in any event.

Ponies.
Penalty 8.

(b) A pony blind of an eye may not be played; a pony showing vice, or not under proper control, shall not be allowed in the game.

Equipment Prohibited. Shoeing Restrictions.
Penalty 8.

2.—Blinkers, sharp spurs, and shadow rolls are not allowed nor are protruding buckles or studs on a player's boots or knee pads.

3.—Dull heel calks of standard type are allowed only on the heels of hind shoes. Not allowed are shoes with an outer rim, toe grab, screws, or frost nails.

Ground Kept Clear.

4.—No person or persons shall be allowed within the playing field and safety zone except Players, Umpires, Referee, Manager, Stick-holders and Goal Judges, except by special permission of the Umpire.

Infringement a Foul.

5.—Any infringement of the Field Rules and certain of the General Rules constitutes a foul, and the Umpire may stop the game.

Whistle Dead Ball.

6.—(a) The Umpire shall carry a whistle and shall sound it loudly when he decides play shall be stopped. At the moment the Umpire's whistle sounds, the ball is dead. Other than when the Umpire sounds his whistle to end a period, the interval that elapses between the time the Umpire blows his whistle and the resumption of play shall not be deducted from the period, except as otherwise noted in the Rules.

(b) If a whistle is blown for a foul at approximately the same time as a goal is made:

(i) The goal shall *not* be scored if the foul were made by the attacking side and the foul is confirmed.

U. S. P. A. FIELD RULES

(ii) It shall be scored if the foul were made by the attacking side and the foul is over-ruled.

(iii) It also shall be scored if the foul were made by the defending side, whether or not it is confirmed.

How Game Commences

7.—The game begins by both teams taking their position at the centre line and the Umpire bowling the ball, underhand and hard, into the centre of the ground in front of and between the opposing ranks of players, each team being stationary and on its own side of the centre line, no player to stand within 5 yards of the Umpire. The team shall decide by lot which goal each will defend.

Ends Changed.

8.—(a) Ends shall be changed after every goal, except goals awarded by handicap or Penalty No. 1. After a goal has been scored the game shall be resumed from the centre line as prescribed by Field Rule No. 7. The players shall be allowed a reasonable time in which to reach the centre line at a slow canter and take their positions. The team which has lost the toss at the beginning of the game may elect, when the game continues after half time, which goal to defend. In the event that goals are changed under this rule and the next period is to start with a bowl-in or hit-in, the ball shall be put back into play in the same relative part of the field.

Wrong Line-Up.

(b) If the Umpire inadvertently permits lining up the wrong way the responsibility rests with him, and there is no redress; but if at the end of the period no goal has been scored the ends shall then be changed.

Goals, Over Top of Goal Posts.

9.—A goal is gained when a ball passes between the goal posts and across and clear of the back line. If a ball is hit between the imaginary vertical lines produced by the inner surfaces of the goal posts and across and clear of the back line, it shall be scored as a goal.

(NOTE.—A ball hit directly over either goal post shall not be scored because it does not pass between the inner vertical lines they produce.)

Ball Hit Behind by Attacking Side.

10.—If the ball be hit across a team's backline by the opposing team, the team whose back line is crossed shall hit the ball in, or hit at it, from a point within one foot on the field where the ball crossed its back line. Should this point be closer than 12 feet to a side board or goal post, the ball shall be hit in, or hit at, from a point 12 feet on the back line from that side board or goal post (but not from between the goal posts). Each team shall be given a reasonable time to position itself for the continuation of play, but no member of the team defending against the hit in shall be closer than 30 yards to that back line when the Umpire says 'Play' and the ball is hit, or hit at.

If a player defending against the hit in is closer than 30 yards to that back line when the Umpire says 'Play' and the ball is hit, or hit at, the Umpire may stop the game and resume it in the same manner. In such a case, the time that elapses between the stoppage of the game and its resumption shall not be deducted from the period.

If the ball is not hit in, or hit at, when Umpire says 'Play', he shall blow his whistle, stop play, and then shall bowl in the ball between the teams at a right angle to the back line from the point it crossed the back line, and no player shall be within 5 yards of the Umpire when he bowls in the ball. Should the ball have crossed the back line at a point near the side boards or side lines that would not allow both teams to be on the playing field for the bowl in, the Umpire shall bowl in from the nearest

APPENDIX VI

point on the back line that permits both teams to be on the field. For such a bowl in, the team which delayed play shall be on the side of the nearest goal post. The interval that elapses between the stoppage and resumption of play shall be deducted from the period.

Ball Hit Across Back Line.
Penalty 6.

11.—If a player hits the ball behind his own back line, either directly or after glancing off his own pony, or after glancing off the side boards, Penalty No. 6 shall be exacted. If the ball strikes any other player or his pony before crossing that back line, the ball shall be hit in as laid down in Field Rule No. 10.

Ball Out.

12.—(a) The ball must go across and clear of the side boards, side lines, or back lines to be out.

Ball Bowled In by Umpire.

(b) When the ball is hit across the side boards or side lines, it must be bowled, underhand and hard, by the Umpire into the ground from a point just inside the boards or lines where it went out, on a line parallel to the two back lines, and in front of and between the opposing ranks of players, each side being on its own side of the line, no player to stand within 5 yards of the Umpire. A reasonable time must be allowed the players in which to line up.

Ball Put in Play

13.—In all cases when the Umpire puts the ball into play by bowling it in between the teams, the Umpire shall be on the playing field and each team stationary on its own side, with no player being within 5 yards of the Umpire, and the Umpire shall bowl the ball hard into the ground in front of and between the teams in a direction parallel to the back lines, except as in Field Rule No. 10.

(a) If the ball is hit across the side boards or side lines, the Umpire shall bowl in the ball from a point just inside the boards or lines where it went out and toward the opposite boards or lines.

(b) If the ball hits the boards without going over them, ending a period, and there being other periods remaining in the game, the ball shall be bowled in as if it had been hit across the boards.

(c) If the Umpire stops play while the ball is on the playing field, he shall resume play by bowling in the ball at the point toward the nearer side boards or side lines. In the event this point does not allow sufficient room for the teams to line up on the field, the Umpire shall bowl in the ball in the same manner from the nearest point that allows it.

(d) If the side fouled awarded a free hit under a penalty does not hit, or hit at, the ball in a reasonable time after the Umpire says 'Play', the Umpire shall bowl in the ball between the teams toward either side boards or side lines, the decision to be his and to be final, and he shall bowl it in at the point it was placed for the free hit.

(e) If the ball is not hit in, or hit at, on a hit in from the back line in a reasonable time after the Umpire says 'Play', the Umpire shall blow his whistle, stop play, and shall bowl in the ball between the teams as laid down in Field Rule No. 10.

(f) In case of a Penalty No. 1, the Umpire shall bowl in the ball from a point 10 yards perpendicular to the centre of the fouling side's goal, positioning himself with that side's back line to his right.

Damaged Ball, etc.

14.—(a) Should a ball break in such a manner as not to be playable when first struck on a free hit awarded under a penalty, or on a hit-in, the game shall be stopped by the Umpire and resumed from the same point with another ball in the same manner. Time which elapses during this stoppage shall be deducted from the period.

U. S. P. A. FIELD RULES

(b) Other than as set forth in the foregoing paragraph (a), if the ball becomes damaged to the extent it is unplayable by being chipped, broken, or trodden into the ground, the Umpire, at his discretion, shall stop play and bowl in another ball as near as possible to the point of play when his whistle sounded. Time during these stoppages shall not be deducted from the period.

(c) What is a chipped, broken, buried, or unplayable ball in the two foregoing paragraphs shall be the sole discretion of the Umpire.
(NOTE.—For the purposes of subsection (b) of this Rule, if the ball be minorly chipped or broken, the Umpire should not stop play until it is in such a position that neither side is favoured).

15.—A player may not catch, kick or hit the ball with anything but his stick. He may block it with any part of his body. He may not carry the ball intentionally. If the ball becomes lodged against a player, his pony or its equipment, in such a way that it cannot be dropped immediately, the Umpire shall blow his whistle and bowl the ball in at the point where it was first carried. **Carrying Ball, etc.** *Penalty 5.*

16.—At each moment of the game there shall exist a right of way. No player may cross another player who has the right of way or enter into the right of way except at such a distance as does not involve the possibility of collision or danger to either player. No player may enter on a new line immediately if there is a risk of collision with a player following the previous line. **Crossing.** *Penalty 2, 3, 4 or 5.*

(a) The right of way gives a player the right to hit the ball on the off side of his pony. If he places himself so as to hit it on the near side of his pony, he must give way to the player making a play that would have been without danger had he stayed on his proper side. If two players are riding from opposite directions to hit the ball each shall hit the ball on the off side of his pony. *Penalty 2, 3, 4 or 5.*

(b) That player has the right of way who is riding in the direction in which it was hit, on, or at the least angle to the line of the ball, except as against a player who is riding to meet the ball on the exact line of its course. **Right of Way.**

(c) If two players are riding from different directions to hit the ball and a dangerous collision appears probable, the player who has the right of way must be given way to. **Right of Way.** *Penalty 2, 3, 4 or 5.*

(d) Any player who rides to meet the ball on exact line of its course has the right of way rather than any other player riding at an angle from any direction. **Rider to Meet It.**

(e) A player riding in the direction in which the ball is travelling, at an angle to its line, has the right of way over a player riding to meet the ball, at an angle to its line, irrespective of the width of the angles.

(f) Two players, only when following the line of the ball attempting to ride one another off, has the right of way over a single player coming from any direction. **Right of Way.** *Penalty 2, 3, 4 or 5.*

(g) As between players riding to meet the ball, that player has the right of way whose course is at the least angle to the line of the ball.

(h) No player may enter the line of the ball in front of a player who has the right of way except at such a distance as does not involve the possibility of collision or danger to either player. The line of the ball, for the purposes of this paragraph, means the line the ball has travelled *Penalty 2, 3, 4 or 5.*

APPENDIX VI

and not the line of the ball produced. If a player enters safely on the line of the ball, a player may not ride into him from behind but must take the ball on the near side of his own pony.

(*i*) No player shall be deemed to have the right of way by reason of his being the last striker, if he shall have deviated from pursuing the exact line of the ball. In such a case, the right of way shall be determined by the other paragraphs of this article. (*See Appendix, Example I.*)

Penalty 2, 3, 4 or 5.

(*j*) No player may pull up across the line of the ball if by doing so he endangers himself or a player who has the right of way.

Penalty 2, 3, 4 or 5.

(*k*) In the rare case of two players riding in the general direction of the ball at exactly equal angles to it on opposite sides of its line, the right of way belongs to that player who has the line of the ball on his off side. The same rule applies as between players meeting the ball on exactly equal angles from opposite sides of this line.

(*l*) If the ball becomes stationary while remaining in play, the line of the ball is that line it was travelling before stopping.

Line of the Ball.

(NOTE.—The line of the ball is the line of its course or that line produced at the moment any question arises, unless otherwise provided.

When the ball has been put in play by being hit at, the line of the ball shall be the direction in which the player was riding when he hit at the ball.)

Dangerous Riding.
Penalty 2, 3, 4 or 10

17.—A player may ride off an opponent or may interpose his pony between an opponent and the ball but he may not ride dangerously, as for example:

(*a*) Bumping in a manner dangerous to a player or his pony.

(*b*) Zigzagging in front of another player riding at a gallop.

(*c*) Pulling across or over a pony's fore or hind legs in such a manner as to risk tripping the pony.

(*d*) Riding an opponent across the line of the ball as specified in Example V.

(*e*) Lack of consideration for safety on the part of a player for himself, his pony, or for other players and their ponies.

(*f*) Two players of the same team riding-off an opponent at the same time whether or not it being on the right of way.

Rough Play.
Penalty 2, 3, 4, 5 or 10.

18.—No player may seize with the hand, strike, or push with the head, hand, arm, or elbow, but a player may push with his arm, above the elbow, provided the elbow be kept close to his side.

Penalty 2, 3, 4 or 5

19.—(*a*) No player may hook or strike an opponent's stick unless he is on the same side of the opponent's pony as the ball, or in a direct line behind, and his stick is neither over, nor under the body or across the legs of the opponent's pony. The stick may not be hooked or struck unless the adversary is in the act of striking at the ball. The act of striking at the ball shall include both the upward and downward phases of the stroke. No player may hook or strike an opponent's stick above shoulder level, nor may he use his stick in a manner dangerous to another player, his own, or another player's pony.

Penalty 2, 3, 4 or 5

(*b*) No player may reach immediately over and across or under and across any part of an opponent's pony to strike at the ball, nor may he hit into or among the legs of an opponent's pony nor deliberately ride his own pony into the stroke of another player.

160

U. S. P. A. FIELD RULES

(c) No player may intentionally strike his pony with the head or the butt of his polo stick. **Striking Pony with Head of Stick.** *Penalty 5*

(d) No player may use his stick dangerously. *Penalty 2, 3, 4, 5 or 10*

20.—A player requiring a stick, a change of pony, or assistance from an outside person during a game shall ride beyond the end lines or side boards or side lines to procure it. No person shall come onto the playing ground to assist him, except when the ball is dead and when permission is granted by the Umpire. **No Outside Assistance on Ground.** *Penalty 5*

21.—No dismounted player may hit the ball or interfere in the game. **Dismounted Player.** *Penalty 2, 3, 4 or 10.*

22.—(a) If a pony falls or be injured, the Umpire shall stop play. A player whose pony has been injured shall change to another pony within 5 minutes, providing the Umpire deems the injury to be of a serious nature. Play shall be resumed immediately, if the injury is decided not severe, and not later than 5 minutes if the change of pony is allowed. **Accidents.**

(b) If any part of a pony's gear becomes broken or unfastened and there is a possibility it could cause an accident, the Umpire shall stop play immediately and allow that player to make the necessary repairs or replacements before re-starting the play. In this case, the player may not change ponies. In the case of broken or unfastened tack that does not present a dangerous situation, the player shall notify the Umpire when the ball next goes out of play. The Umpire shall then stop the game and give the player an opportunity to make necessary repairs or adjustments to the tack before he re-starts the game. Also, in this case, the player may not change ponies.

(c) In the event of an accident to a player, the Umpire shall stop the game and the player shall have 15 minutes within which to return to the game. If and when during this interval the injured player is able to return to play or an eligible player is substituted for him, the Umpire shall resume play. Play shall not be resumed later than 15 minutes after it was stopped because of the accident. A player who leaves the game because of injury shall not be eligible to return to the game.

(d) If a player falls off his pony, the Umpire shall not stop the game until the ball is next out of play. If, however, the player, in the opinion of the Umpire, is injured, or in jeopardy of being injured, the Umpire shall stop play immediately.

(e) What constitutes a fall shall be left to the discretion of the Umpire.

23.—If a player be disabled by a foul so that he is unable to continue, Penalty 7 may be exacted, or the side which has been fouled shall have the option of providing a substitute. **Disablement by Foul.** *Penalty 2, 7 or 10.*

24.—(a) Should any incident or question not provided for in these General or Field Rules arise in a match, such incident or question shall be decided by the Umpire or Umpires. If the Umpires disagree, the Referee's decision shall be final. **Incidents Not Provided for by Rules.**

(b) There are degrees of dangerous play and of unfair play, as it confers an advantage to the side fouling, or a disadvantage to the side fouled. Where more than one penalty is prescribed in the margins to the Rules, the penalty or penalties to be inflicted is left to the discretion of

APPENDIX VI

the Umpire. It shall be within the discretion of the Umpire not to stop the game and inflict a penalty if the stopping of the game and the infliction of the penalty would be a disadvantage to the side which had been fouled.

PENALTIES

(NOTE.—More than one of these penalties may be exacted by the Umpire when applicable.)

1.—(a) If, in the opinion of the Umpire, a player commits a dangerous or deliberate foul in the vicinity of his team's goal in order to save a goal, the side fouled shall be awarded one goal and ends shall not be changed.

(b) The game shall be resumed by the ball being bowled in parallel to the back lines from a point 10 yards perpendicular to the centre of the fouling side's goal, the Umpire positioning himself in front of and facing the players, with the fouling side's back line to his right.

2.—(a) A free hit at the ball by the side fouled from a point 30 yards perpendicular to the centre of the fouling side's goal, or, if preferred by the Captain of the side fouled, from the point the foul occurred. All of the fouling side shall position themselves behind their back line, and they shall not come onto the playing field until the Umpire says 'Play' and the ball is hit, or hit at, and then not from between the goal posts. The side fouled shall not be closer to that back line than the ball when it is hit, or hit at.

(b) If in the opinion of the Umpire the free hit would have resulted in a score, but was prevented by the fouling side's coming onto the playing field from between the goal posts or across the back line before play re-started, a goal shall be scored.

(c) If the fouling side fails to carry out the proper procedure and no goal was scored as a result of the free hit, the side fouled shall be awarded another free hit at the ball from the same point under the same conditions.

(d) If the side fouled fails to carry out the proper procedure, the fouling side shall hit the ball in, or hit at it, from the centre of its back line between the goal posts, with no member of the side fouled closer than 30 yards of the back line when the ball is hit, or hit at.

(e) If both sides fail to carry out the proper procedure, the side fouled shall have another free hit at the ball from the same point under the same conditions.

3.—(a) A free hit at the ball by the side fouled from a point 40 yards perpendicular to the centre of the fouling side's goal. All of the fouling side shall position themselves behind their back line, and they shall not come onto the playing field until the Umpire says 'Play' and the ball is hit, or hit at, and then not from between the goal posts. The side fouled shall not be closer to the back line than the ball when it is hit, or hit at.

(b) Same as Penalty No. 2 (b)
(c) Same as Penalty No. 2 (c)
(d) Same as Penalty No. 2 (d)
(e) Same as Penalty No. 2 (e)

4.—(a) A free hit at the ball by the side fouled from a point 60 yards perpendicular to the centre of the fouling side's goal, both sides free to

U.S.P.A. PENALTIES

position themselves anywhere on or off the playing field except that no member of the fouling side shall be closer than 30 yards of the ball when the Umpire says 'Play' and the ball is hit, or hit at.

(b) If the fouling side fails to carry out the proper procedure and no goal is scored as a result of the free hit, the side fouled shall be awarded another free hit at the ball from the same point under the same conditions.

5.—(a) A free hit at the ball by the side fouled from the point the foul occurred, or from the centre of the playing field, the decision to be made by the Umpire, both sides free to position themselves anywhere on or off the playing field, except that no member of the fouling side shall be closer than 30 yards of the ball when the Umpire says 'Play' and the ball is hit, or hit at.

(b) Same as Penalty No. 4 (b).

6.—(a) A free hit at the ball by the side fouled from a point 60 yards perpendicular to where the ball crossed the back line, both sides free to position themselves anywhere on or off the playing field except that no member of the fouling side shall be closer than 30 yards of the ball when the Umpire says 'Play' and the ball is hit, or hit at.

(b) Same as Penalty No. 4 (b).

7.—If a player is disabled by a foul to the exent the Umpire permits or orders his retirement from the game, the Captain of the side fouled shall designate the removal of a player from the fouling side whose handicap is nearest above, even with, or lesser than that of the disabled player. If the disabled player's handicap is higher than that of any player on the fouling side, any member of that team may be designated. In the event of a handicap tournament or match, there shall be no change in the handicap from as it was at the commencement of the game.

8.—The pony ordered off the ground by the Umpire and disqualified from being played again during the game or match. If a pony is ordered off the ground for infringement of Field Rule No. 3, after removal of offense, the pony may be allowed to play provided the game is not delayed.

9.—The match shall be forfeited.

10.—The Umpire may exclude a player for all or any portion of the remaining periods of a game, in case of a deliberate, dangerous foul, or conduct prejudicial to the game, and he may, or may not, allow a substitution for the removed player during the exclusion. In the event substitution is allowed, that player shall be of even or lesser handicap, and there shall be no change in the handicap from as it was at the commencement of the game.

Intent for Use Of.

Penalty No. 5 (a) is for MINOR infractions, play of a nature that is not deliberate and does not risk injury to players or ponies but that does confer a minor advantage to the fouling side, or a minor disadvantage to the side fouled—or both. These are fouls such as: an inadvertent cross hook; placing a mallet over or under the body or across the legs of an opponent's pony at slow play; crossing another player coming on the right of way at slow speed; a player's impeding play by being on the right of way at a point of play without knowing it, or, knowing it, being unable to clear himself from the line in the proper time. These same infractions, however, can be MAJOR if they have a MAJOR effect on the game, depending on their location and the circumstances surrounding them.

Under Penalty No. 5 (a), if a team commits a MINOR infraction in its half of the field, the free hit should be given from the centre of the

APPENDIX VI

field. If, however, a side is fouled MINORLY in its opponent's half of the field, the free hit should be awarded from the point the infraction occurred.

U. S. P. A. EXAMPLES

EXAMPLES OF FIELD RULES
EXAMPLE I

Field Rule 16 (*i*).—Deviation from line of ball.

B, on the ball, hits to X, and swings around in a semicircle. A, on a good polo pony, is following the line of the ball.

At A' B' a collision is imminent.

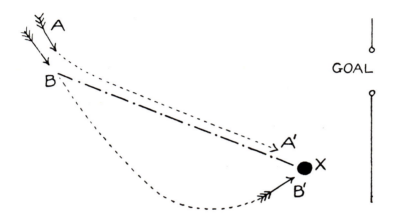

Although B hit the ball last, he loses the right of way, because A has ridden on a line closer and more nearly parallel to the line on which the ball has been travelling.

A has the right of way and must be given way to.

APPENDIX VI

EXAMPLE II

Field Rule 16.—Crossing.
Field Rule 16.—Right of way.

A hits the ball in from behind to *X*.
B rides to meet it, and *C* to take it on.

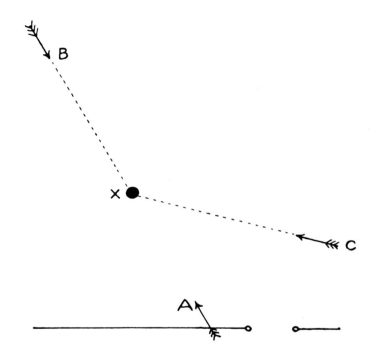

A collision is imminent between *B* and *C* at *X*.

B must be given way to, because he is on the line on which the ball travels, even though coming in an opposite direction, whereas *C* would cross that line.

U. S. P. A. EXAMPLES

EXAMPLE III
Field Rule 16.—Crossing.

A hits the ball to X.

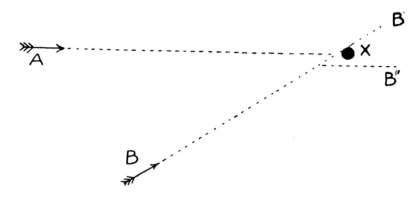

If B can unquestionably reach the ball at X, without fouling, then B can take an off-side backhander at B'.

But if there is reasonable doubt, then it is B's duty to swerve towards B" (the line of the ball), and take a near side backhander, and if in taking that backhander, or afterward, his pony in the slightest degree crosses the line of the ball, a 'cross' should be given against him.

APPENDIX VI

EXAMPLE IV

Field Rule 16.—Crossing.
Field Rule 16 (*b*).—Right of way.
Field Rule 16 (*c*).—Riding at smallest angle.

The ball has been hit to *X*.
Neither *A* nor *B* hit it there.

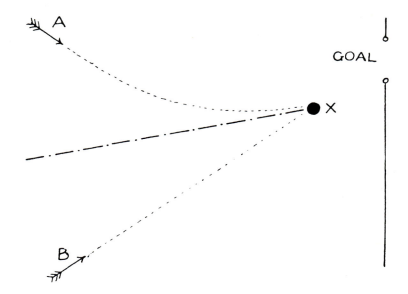

Both start to ride to the ball with equal rights. A collision is probable at *X*. *A* must be given way to, as he has followed more closely the line on which the ball has been travelling.

U. S. P. A. EXAMPLES

EXAMPLE V

Field Rule 17 (*d*)

No. 2 (Red), hits to *X*.

All three players ride for the ball, No. 1 (Red) riding off the back (Blue) all the way, and a collision between the three is imminent at *X*.

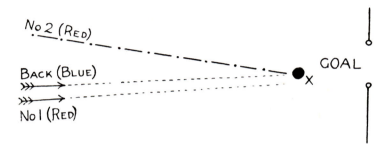

No. 2 (Red) has the right of way.

A dangerous foul should be given against No. 1 (Red) if he causes the back to cross No. 2 or if he causes the back to pull up so as to avoid a collision with the No. 2.

APPENDIX VII
THE UNITED STATES POLO ASSOCIATION GUIDE FOR UMPIRES

Classification of Umpires (and Referees).

1.—As a primary means toward obtaining the highest quality and uniformity of officials for various events, an umpire classification system has been derived as an aid in selecting knowledgeable officials. These classifications are as follows:

(a) National Class—Qualified to officiate any tournament or match; Club, Circuit, National or International.

(b) A Class—Qualified to officiate 0 through 22 goal polo.

(c) B Class—Qualified to officiate 0 through 14 goal polo.

(d) C Class—Qualified to officiate 0 through 8 goal polo.

Selection of Umpires.

2.—(a) The following is a recommendation for selecting officials for specific classifications of events. In all cases, emphasis should be placed upon obtaining the highest classified officials possible, regardless of the event. Below are recommended minimums.

(i) For International Tournaments of Cup of The Americas Class—all officials (2 mounted umpires, referee) should be National Class.

(ii) For National or U.S.P.A. sponsored events:

A   United States Handicap, Open, Gold Cup, Silver Cup, America Cup—at least one National Class umpire and one A Class umpire. A Class referee.

B   Continental Cup—one A Class umpire, one B Class umpire. B Class referee.

C   Chairman's Cup, Inter-Circuit—one A Class umpire, one B Class umpire. B Class referee.

D   Delegate's Cup, President's Cup—Both umpires B Class. C Class referee.

E   Intra-Circuit—Both umpires B Class. B Class referee.

F   Circuit President's Cup—Both umpires B Class. C Class referee.

Remember, the above are minimum standards for officials. If at all possible obtain officials of higher classification than suggested.

(b) Umpires and referees should, whenever possible, have no affiliation with any team or team member playing in the event. National Class umpires may be considered exceptions to this rule.

(NOTE.—By excepting National Class umpires, it is in no way a reflection upon the integrity of those in other classifications, but is simply a matter of expedience since such a relatively small number of officials fall into the National Class, to exclude any, at any time, might cause inconvenience in obtaining the best qualified people.)

(c) When possible for the America Cup, Silver Cup, Gold Cup, U.S. Handicap and Open, one of the umpires (i.e. the same man) should officiate all games in the tournament as this establishes a uniformity throughout the event.

U. S. P. A. GUIDE FOR UMPIRES

Proper Attire or Uniform.

3.—Too often, particularly on the Club and Circuit level, but to some extent on the National level, there is a wide variance in uniform worn by the umpires on the field. The result being that frequently spectators, and even players, experience a certain difficulty in quickly identifying the officials. Therefore, for ease of identification, and in some cases attendant safety reasons, the following should be the proper uniform for umpires:

(a) Khaki, tan, canary or white breeches (not jeans or chaps).

(b) Black and white vertical stripe shirts—long or short sleeve.

(c) Suitable cap or hat may be worn (a cap is to be preferred). Straw or felt wide brimmed 'Cowboy' or 'Planter' style hats should not be worn for safety reasons. (Too often a wide brimmed hat may blow off, either scaring a horse or causing unnecessary delay while it is being retrieved.)

(d) Good audible whistle and ball bag. Pick-up sticks are optional. (Each umpire should have both a whistle and ball bag.)

Duties Before the Game

4.—To insure that the match progresses as smoothly as possible for the benefit of all concerned, the officials should be responsible in the following matters:

(a) The referee should be placed by himself (alone) at a proper vantage point, preferably at an elevated position along the sidelines but in the centre of the field so that the umpires may readily locate him for consultation and that he may have, as near as possible, an unobstructed view of the playing field. The task of the referee is a very responsible one, and requires continual concentration throughout the game. The referee should, therefore, have had considerable polo experience, and, if possible in umpiring. He should not only know the rules well, but should be able to refer to any rule quickly. In this regard, the referee should always be supplied with, and keep at hand, the Blue Book.

(b) If, in the opinion of two of the officials, the third would not be able to competently carry out his duties, they should request that the tournament committee appoint a substitute.

(c) Umpires should consult with flagmen (and Goal officials if any) to be certain that they are aware of their duties and that an adequate supply of new polo balls is available at each end of the field.

(d) Umpires should check with the respective team captains to ascertain if team uniforms are easily distinguishable. If not, the tournament committee should be informed and the matter decided according to General Rule 10.

(e) Umpires are responsible to see that the General Rules governing players and ponies and pony equipment are adhered to. (Example: The umpire should make a cursory check to see that sharp spurs, shadow rolls, etc. are not being used.)

(f) Officials should refrain from consuming alcoholic beverages both before and during the game. (It is only fair to the competing teams that the officials in no way restrict themselves from performing as efficiently as possible.)

(g) Instructions to team captains and choosing direction of play should be done ten minutes prior to the commencement of the game.

(h) The umpires should, fifteen (15) minutes prior to the commencement of the game, ascertain that the timekeeper is in his proper position;

APPENDIX VII

that the clock is in proper working order; and that the scoreboard and scoreboard operator are properly prepared.

(*i*) —It is the responsibility of the umpires to see that the game begins on time. To that effect, he should sound his whistle five minutes prior to the commencement of the game and again two minutes prior to the commencement of the game at which time all players should be on the field of play. During this two minute interval between the second whistle and the throw-in, the umpires should give any necessary last minute instructions to the players. There must be a valid reason to delay the game, otherwise the game should be started promptly on time whether all the players are on the field or not.

General Practice for Officials During the Game.

5.—(*a*) Line-ups preparatory to throw in

(i) (It should be pre-determined, between the umpires, which will throw-in.) The umpire throwing-in should require the players to keep a five yard distance from his (the umpire's) mount before the ball is put in play.

(ii) The second umpire (who is not throwing-in) should place himself directly behind the line-up. (It is this umpire's primary responsibility to look for and call any fouls which might occur during the scrimmage resulting from the throw-in.)

(iii) When throwing-in, the umpire should always bowl the ball, between the line of players, hard and underhand.

(NOTE.—The ball should be on the ground by the time it reaches the number 1's. Do not throw the ball overhand or side arm or outside the centre of the line-up.)

(iv) When the ball goes over the side boards, the umpire throwing-in must be sure he places his mount inside the boards, on the playing field, before he bowls the ball in to resume play.

(v) If the umpire responsible for the throw-in, has trouble with his mount at the throw-in, he should not waste time but promptly change positions with the second umpire who should then proceed with the throw-in. In cases where there is only one umpire, and he encounters difficulty with his mount at the throw-in, he should sound his whistle to stop the clock, and change mounts. If there are two umpires, and the delay appears to be protracted, the game should be stopped (by the umpire's whistle) until positions can be changed and the throw-in properly conducted.

(NOTE.—As a general rule, the players should not be penalised by a delay caused by the umpires; however, should the players fail to promptly and properly align themselves for a throw-in, then that resultant delay shall rest with them.)

(vi) The umpire throwing in may require the teams to realign themselves as he deems necessary.

(*b*)—Procedures while the ball is in play

(i) It is very important (mandatory) that umpires be very prompt in blowing their whistles to stop play, whether a foul has been committed or other reasons dictate such action.

(A) At the moment the umpire's whistle sounds, the ball is dead. (Field Rule No. 6.) There have been instances in the past, and will be in the future, where a player scores a goal and one umpire calls a foul against the scoring side. The other umpire disagrees and the referee is consulted.

The referee rules no foul. Should the goal stand or be taken away? The Umpire Committee feels that the umpire's whistle should be the controlling factor. If, in the opinion of the umpire(s) the whistle sounded before the ball passed through the goal then the ball was dead at that point and no goal should be allowed. Play should be resumed with the ball bowled in facing the near boards at the point where the ball was whistled dead. But, if in the opinion of the umpire(s) the ball was through the goal before the whistle sounded and no foul is ruled, then the goal should stand.

(ii) During play, both umpires should maintain the pace of the game and place themselves as close to the play as possible without interfering with the players.

(iii) One umpire should place himself near the forward end of the play and the other should follow the play. By so spacing themselves, they will have a better perspective of the play at any given moment. If there is only one umpire, it is generally more satisfactory to follow the play rather than advance before it.

(A) As an alternative method to the above placement procedures, the following has been employed with some success. Essentially, umpires should divide the field in half and patrol in the main their half of the field. If a line were drawn from the mid-point of each goal, the umpires can then divide the field and position themselves as well as possible to the movement of the ball up and down the field. Both, therefore, will be close to the play, viewing it from different angles and opposite sides. This coordinated plan requires that the umpires move aggressively up and down the field and always be within 50 or so yards of the play.

(iv) Umpires should guard against riding close together or parallel to one another or to the play as the best vantage point is as near up or down the line of the ball and the flow of play as possible. Umpires should also bear in mind that it is easier to observe the play if they place themselves between the sun and the play.

(c) Procedures and placement for a knock-in

(i) When the ball goes over the back line, one umpire with deliberate speed shall see that the flagman properly positions the ball and when the teams have positioned themselves, shall call 'play'.

(NOTE.—The ball should not be struck or struck at unless the umpire does, in fact, call 'play'. The umpire may call 'play' at his discretion, and shall give the teams adequate, but not undue, time to position themselves for the knock-in.

(ii) The umpire closest to the ball shall be responsible for calling 'play'.

(iii) Regardless whether the situation is a knock-in or a penalty (free) shot, when the umpire calls 'play', should a player on the attacking side (or side fouled) touch or move the ball with his mallet, whether or not he is the player making the shot, the ball is then in play.

(iv) On a knock-in, one umpire should place himself in the vicinity of the ball, without interfering with the players, and the other should place himself approximately seventy (70) yards from the back line on the same side of the field as the ball is placed for the knock-in.

APPENDIX VII

(d) Procedures and placement for penalties

(i) Penalties 2 and 3 (penalty 1 is the same as 3 except that a goal is awarded as well as a free shot from 40 yards)—one umpire shall place himself on the back line to make sure no player on the defending side crosses the back line before the ball is hit or hit at. The other umpire shall place himself in the vicinity of the ball, in such position so as to afford himself an unobstructed view of the goal, on a line with the line of the ball.

(ii) For penalties 4, 5 and 6, one umpire should place himself behind the defending team (which, in the case of penalties 4 and 6, will be behind the goal line) while the other umpire should place himself in the vicinity of the ball.

(e) Consultation between Umpires and Referee

When there is disagreement between the umpires as to whether or not a foul occurred or as to which team committed the foul they should proceed directly to the referee. Each umpire should briefly state his opinion and the referee should, as quickly as possible deliver his decision. Example: Umpire A calls a foul on Red for crossing. Umpire B disagrees on the basis there was no danger involved. They ride to the referee at which time Umpire A explains (briefly) his call. Umpire B then explains (briefly) his reason(s) for disagreeing. The referee, based on what he observed then either allows the foul or rules no foul. The referee should not allocate a penalty unless the umpires should agree on the foul but disagree on the penalty to be awarded.

Authority of the Umpires.

6.—(a) The umpires shall have, and maintain, absolute authority, and control of the game at all times. The umpires' (and referee's if consulted) decision shall be final and not subject to discussion on the part of the players. If a question arises, it may be communicated by the team captain only. This applies to questionable goals (i.e. whether or not a goal was scored regardless of the flagman's signal) as well and in this case, as in all other questions arising from play, the umpires' and/or referee's (if consulted) decision is final. The umpires and/or referee (if consulted) can over-rule the opinion of the flagman or the goal judge regarding whether or not the goal was scored. At the umpire's discretion, a warning may be issued, or a fine or fines not to exceed $50 may be assessed a player during a game for any form of misconduct. The umpire, may also, increase the severity of a penalty, i.e. change the penalty from a 4 to a 3 and so on, if he deems such action necessary to maintaining control of the game. The umpires may, in addition to the above referenced disciplinary measures, eject a player from the game and also, may, with the concurrence of the Tournament Committee responsible for the tournament being played, submit to the U.S.P.A. Board of Governors a written recommendation of suspension for any period of time, for the player or players involved in misconduct deemed detrimental to the game. (See Field Rules, Penalty 10.)

(b) See Field Rule 24

Criteria for Determining Severity of Penalties.

7.—(a) Penalty 5

(i) One of the most useful yet misunderstood penalties is the Penalty 5. The Penalty 5 gives the side fouled a free hit from the spot where the foul occurred or from the centre of the ground, the decision resting with the umpires. Generally, the Penalty 5 is awarded for less severe fouls such as an accidental cross hook, hitting into or across a pony's legs, elbowing, striking a pony with the mallet or less severe crossing infractions, but it may be awarded at any time at the umpire's discretion. As a general, but not mandatory guideline, if the side fouled is in its end of the field (the end it is defending) and a Penalty 5 is called, the free hit should be from centre ground. Likewise, if the side fouled is in the opponents end of the field (the end it is attacking) the free hit should be from the point of the infraction. The umpires should, prior to the game, discuss the basis on which a Penalty 5 will be awarded from centre ground or from the point of infraction and make their calls accordingly. There should be consistency in the awarding of Penalty 5's.

(b) —Penalty 4

(i) Probably the most common penalty and justifiably so, it may be called for a foul committed anywhere on the field. Generally, however, if a foul occurs within the 60 yard line of the fouling side where the attacking player has a clear shot at goal, a Penalty 1, 2 or 3 should be called. If the foul is within the 60 yard line of the fouling side, but is not so severe as to award a Penalty 1, 2 or 3 and is at a point on the field where the attacking player has little chance of scoring a goal, then a Penalty 4 should be called. On the other hand, if the side attacking commits a severe foul in the end of the field it is attacking, a Penalty 5 should not be awarded, but rather a Penalty 4. Example: Red is bringing in from its back line. The Blue No. 1 badly fouls the Red No. 3 who is bringing in, a Penalty 4 should be enacted against the Blue side. If the umpires are in doubt as whether to call a Penalty 4 or Penalty 5, it is generally proper to call a 4 as in some cases a Penalty 5 may in fact be a disadvantage to the side fouled. Example: Red attacking near centre ground with its No. 3 on the ball, its Nos. 1 and 2 out front and only the Blue Back between the Red players and the goal. The Blue Back fouls. To call a Penalty 5 from the centre of the ground would not materially benefit the Red side, and in fact could be construed as a penalty against them, for had the Blue Back not fouled, a Red goal could well have resulted, or at least the Red side would have advanced the ball considerably deeper into Blue's end of the field. To award a Penalty 5 would not only deprive Red of its attack, but would allow all four Blue men to position themselves so as to intercept the resultant Red hit from centre ground. Therefore a Penalty 4 should be given.

(c) —Penalties 2 and 3

(i) As a general, but not arbitrary guideline, if the foul occurs within the 60 yard line in the end of the field the side fouled is attacking, and when the attacking player has a clear shot at goal, either a Penalty 2 or 3 should be awarded. Usually, the closer to the goal and/or the more severe the foul, will determine whether it is a Penalty 2 or 3.

(NOTE.—The umpires should exercise judgement and common sense in allocating fouls in the above referenced area. For example, if the foul occurs within the 60 yard line in the end of the field the side fouled is attacking, but is near the side boards or is of a minor nature, then a Penalty 2 or 3 should in all probability not be awarded, but rather a Penalty 4 or perhaps a Penalty 5 from the spot of the infraction. However, the umpires must maintain consistency in their awarding of penalties. Remember that in the case of a Penalty 2 the side fouled has the option of taking the free hit from either the point of the foul or from the prescribed yard line in front of the goal. When the umpire calls

APPENDIX VII

a Penalty 2, he should ride immediately to the point of the foul and ask the team captain whether the free hit will be taken from that point or from the prescribed yard line.)

(*d*)—Penalty 1

(i) If in the opinion of the umpire a player commits a dangerous or deliberate foul in the vicinity of the goal in order to prevent a score, the side fouled shall be awarded one goal and given a free hit from the 40 yard line as in a Penalty 3. This of course is the most severe penalty and is rarely given, however, the umpires should keep this penalty in mind and award it if they deem it justified.

Definition of Penalty 6 or Safety.

8.—A safety occurs (with the resultant awarding of a Penalty 6) only in the following instance: If a defending player hits the ball behind his own back line and the ball does not, prior to crossing the backline, hit another player, another player's pony, or a goal post, then a Penalty 6 should be given.

(NOTE.—If the defending player hits the ball and it glances off his own pony, or the side boards, then a Penalty 6 should be given. See Field Rule 11.)

APPENDIX VIII

HURLINGHAM POLO ASSOCIATION AND UNITED STATES POLO ASSOCIATION PENALTIES COMPARED

As stated in the History of the Rules (Appendix II) after the International Rules had been drafted by the author in 1938 for the International Rules Committee, in association with the Chairmen of the principal Polo Associations, the United States Polo Association found themselves unable to ratify them. This led to some differences in the wording and numbering of Rules and Penalties, which have persisted when the Hurlingham Polo Association took over the International Rules.

A summary of the Penalties used by both associations is given below. The main differences will be found in Penalties 7, 8 and 9. The U.S.P.A. Penalty 1 automatically includes Penalty 3, and their Penalty 3 can be the same as their Penalty 2 if the Captain of the fouled side elects to take the hit from where the foul occurred.

The H.P.A. Penalty 7 collects the cases of infringements of the Rules in carrying out penalties, whereas the U.S.P.A. leaves particulars under the various penalties. The H.P.A. have no Penalty to forfeit the match corresponding to U.S.P.A. Penalty 9.

In 1938 the author gave every Penalty in the International Rules a short name as well as a number (e.g. Penalty 3—40 Yard Hit) which was not adopted by the U.S.P.A. The most important rule in Polo, Field Rule 16, dealing with 'crossing' was clarified in the H.P.A. rules but in effect has the same intention as U.S.P.A. Field Rule 16.

Really there is no serious discrepancy between the two sets of Rules and Penalties but Players, and even more so Umpires, on crossing the Atlantic, would be well advised to glance at the summary below and then read the full Rules under which they will play or umpire.

HURLINGHAM POLO ASSOCIATION PENALTIES

1. *Penalty Goal.* If a player commits a dangerous or deliberate foul to save a goal, Side fouled receive one goal. Ends not changed. Restart by bowling ball in, 10 yards from middle of Foulers' goal towards either side.
2. *30 Yard Hit.* Ball either 30 yards opposite goal or where foul occurred (fouled Captain's choice). Foulers behind back line, or at least 30 yards from ball; not to ride out through goal. Side fouled behind ball.
3. *40 Yard Hit.* Ball 40 yards opposite goal. Foulers behind back line; not to ride out through goal. Side fouled behind ball.
4. *60 Yard Hit (opposite goal).* Ball 60 yards opposite goal. Foulers to be at least 30 yards from ball; side fouled anywhere.

APPENDIX VIII

5(a)   *Free Hit (from Spot)*. Ball on spot where foul occurred but not within 4 yards of boards or side lines. Foulers to be at least 30 yards from ball; side fouled anywhere.

5(b)   *Free Hit (from Centre)*. Ball in centre of ground. Foulers to be at least 30 yards from ball; side fouled anywhere.

6.   *60 Yard Hit (from where ball crossed)*. Ball on 60 yard line opposite where it crossed back line, but not within 4 yards of boards or side lines. Foulers to be at least 30 yards from ball; side fouled anywhere.

7(a)   *Another Hit*. If Foulers infringe Penalties 2 to 6 carry out penalty again unless goal awarded. If both sides infringe Penalties 2 or 3 carry out penalty again irrespective of result of previous Free Hit.

7(b)   *Hit in by Defenders*. If side fouled infringe Penalties 2 or 3 Defenders hit in from middle of own goal. Attackers to be at least 30 yards from back line; Defenders anywhere.

7(c)   *Hit in from 30 Yard Line*. If attackers cross 30 yard line before a 'Hit in' ball is moved straight forward to 30 yard line and Attackers hit in from there. Attackers to be at least 30 yards from ball; Defenders anywhere.

7(d)   *Unnecessary Delay*. If unnecessary delay by side fouled to take hit, in Penalties 2 to 5, restart game by bowling ball in from previous spot towards side of ground.

8.   *Player to Retire*. Player nearest above handicap of disabled player designated by fouled Captain to retire. Foulers must continue with three players or forfeit match.

9(a)   *Pony Disqualified*. A pony blind of an eye, showing vice or not under proper control is disqualified and ordered off (H.P.A. Field Rule 3).

9(b)   *Pony Ordered Off*. If a pony's equipment infringes H.P.A. Field Rule 4 it is ordered off until offence has been removed.

9(c)   *Player Ordered Off*. If a player infringes H.P.A. Field Rule 5 he is ordered off until he has removed sharp spurs or buckles or studs.

NOTE   In penalties 9(a), (b) and (c) play must be restarted immediately in accordance with Field Rule 25 (*i.e.* ball bowled in towards nearest side from where it was when whistle was blown).

10.   *Player Excluded*. Player ordered off for deliberate dangerous foul or prejudicial conduct. His side must continue with three or forfeit match.

UNITED STATES POLO ASSOCIATION PENALTIES

1.   (a) If player commits dangerous or deliberate foul to save a goal, Side fouled awarded a goal, and given Penalty 3.
    (b) If goal prevented by Foulers infringing rules goal is scored.
    (c) If Foulers infringe rules but no goal was hit Side fouled repeat free hit.
    (d) If Side fouled infringe rules Foulers hit in from centre of goal line; other side at least 30 yards from ball.
    (e) If both Sides infringe rules repeat the penalty.

2.   (a) Ball either 30 yards opposite goal or where foul occurred (fouled Captain's choice). Foulers behind back line or at least 30 yards from ball, not to ride through goal. Side fouled behind ball.
    (b), (c), (d) and (e) same as Penalty 1.

H. P. A. & U. S. P. A. PENALTIES COMPARED

3. Identical with Penalty 2 but for '30 yards' read '40 yards'.
4. (a) Free Hit at ball 60 yards opposite goal. Foulers to be at least 30 yards from ball; Side fouled anywhere.
   (b) If Foulers infringe rules and no goal is scored Side fouled repeat penalty.
5. (a) Free Hit at ball from point where foul occurred or from Centre of Field (Umpire's decision). Foulers to be at least 30 yards from ball; Side fouled anywhere.
   (b) If Foulers infringe rules and no goal is scored Side fouled repeat penalty.

NOTE There are two paragraphs at the end of Penalties dealing with the Intent for use of the two positions of the Ball in Penalty 5.

6. (a) Free Hit at ball on 60 yard line opposite where it crossed back line. Foulers to be at least 30 yards from ball, Side fouled anywhere.
   (b) If Foulers infringe rules and no goal is scored Side fouled repeat penalty.
7. Player nearest above handicap of disabled player designated by fouled Captain to retire. No change in handicap given at start. Foulers must continue with three players or forfeit match.
8. Pony ordered off and disqualified from playing again. If for infringement of U.S.P.A. Field Rule 3 (e.g. heel caulks on front shoes) pony may play again after removal of offence provided game is not delayed.
9. Match forfeited.
10. Player excluded for deliberate dangerous foul or prejudicial conduct. His Side must continue with three.

APPENDIX IX
RULES AND TACTICS

Special Instructions Issued to the United States Polo Squad of 1930

by

Thomas Hitchcock, Jr.

1.—Try as hard as you can all the time. Do not let up for one second, and do not stop until the referee blows his whistle.

2.—Keep your eye on the ball.

3.—Do not dribble the ball. Take a full swing at it every chance you get. There are few exceptions to this rule:

(*a*) When shooting at goal, it is better to miss the ball altogether and leave it in front of the goal, than to hit it over the back-line. Therefore, a dribble or short shot to place the ball in order to make a surer shot at goal is often justifiable.

(*b*) In passing the ball to one of your own side, a short wide pass is often better than a long pass, as it reduces the hazard of an opponent getting the ball.

4.—The player who gets away free with the ball should go at top speed the early part of his run in the hope that he may have a chance to steady himself for the last, most important shot—the shot at goal. The ideal way to make such a run is to make an approach shot that can be picked up at the mouth of goal, about twenty yards from it, thereby greatly facilitating the final shot.

5.—Don't take the ball around by hitting under the pony's neck. There is practically no exception to this rule. A back shot, no matter how feeble, is safer than a shot under the pony's neck which is very difficult to make when going at top speed. A straight forward shot to clear the goal is, of course, advisable. If you must take the ball around, don't make a great wide circle but pivot the pony sharply in as narrow a circle as possible and hit a long shot directly for the opponent's goal.

6.—A man riding to the boards to back the ball in front of his opponent's goal automatically becomes the Back. He should circle his pony so as to cover the back position and he is responsible for the defense until relieved. There is no exception to this rule.

7.—Always play for your own man or the opponent hitting the ball and assume that he will make a good average shot. Try to anticipate this shot at the earliest possible moment and place yourself accordingly. If your opponent has ridden you off, do not pull off or slacken your speed. You are responsible for one man and if you cannot block him, you should hurry him. This is often very effective. Take nothing for granted. That is, if a ball is rolling through your own goal and the chances are all against your being able to stop it, do not assume it will go through.

RULES AND TACTICS

It may hit a lump of dirt and slow up enough so that you can get your mallet on it. If you can think of nothing better to do, put your opponent out of position. This applies especially to the One who has more leisure than the others.

8.—Don't leave the ball unless a man on your own side shouts to you to leave it. When you are told to leave the ball, leave it as quickly as possible and ride off your opponent as wide and clear of the play as you can. Don't tell one of your own men to leave it because you have an easier shot at the ball than he, if he has a fair shot on either side of the pony. This holds good except when in front of your opponent's goal. Then you should tell one of your own men to leave it if you have an easier shot for goal than he has.

9.—Play the man rather than the ball. The ball won't travel by itself if you eliminate the man. This is especially important when a man is trying to dribble the ball behind you. All you need do is to check and bump into him hard and that will spoil his play.

INDIVIDUAL PLAY

In placing himself for a play, the One should be a great optimist. The Two should be optimistic but not unduly. The Three should be on the pessimistic side and the Back should be a conservative pessimist. In other words, if the One sees that his Back is going to make a back shot, he should gamble that the shot will be considerably better than the Back's average back shot and place himself accordingly. The Two should place himself for a slightly better than average shot. The Three should expect the Back to miss the ball and cover the opponents' Two.

Conversely, when the Back and Three see that an opponent is about to hit the ball, they should expect a better than average shot and place themselves accordingly. The line of the demarcation between the offensive and the defensive side is drawn between the Two and Three.

The One Position—The ideal One should be two men. He should be on both sides of his Back so that when the game reverses he is always in the right position. This is obviously impossible. The One is the spear head of the attack. He has more opportunities than any man on his side of getting off alone with the ball. This is a scoring position and he should gamble to get himself in that position. If he is right a small percentage of the time he will be a very effective One. The One should be offside of his Back most of the time and he is not responsible for his Back's forward shot except when the Back is within scoring distance of goal.

The Two Position—The Two should be the most active and aggressive man on the side. He should have his nose in every play and be continually forcing the attack. If he is covered by the opposing Three he should not try to meet the Three's back shots but should forge ahead and try to hurry the play. He should look for passes from his Back and Three and when he sees that either one of them is going to back the ball he should call either 'Centre' or 'Boards' to indicate to which side his Back or Three should hit the ball. A pass to the centre of the field is far more effective than a pass to the side boards.

The Three Position—The first thought of the Three should be to cover or block the opposing Two. The Three should usually keep himself on the defensive

APPENDIX IX

side of the opposing Two and be constantly prepared when the game is reversed to ride the Two out of the play. The Three should always cover the Back when the Back has a chance to meet the ball and should generally encourage the Back to come through by giving the Back a sense of security so that he can meet the ball or by playing short wide passes so that the Back can pick it up with a forward shot. The Three should block the opposing Two when his own side is knocking in, and prevent him from meeting the ball.

The Back Position—The Back is responsible for the defense. He should be careful that the opposing One does not slip out ahead of him and get a free run for goal. His most effective play is to turn a defensive situation into an attack. This he can do either by a long back shot, by meeting a ball or by picking up a pass from the Three or Two and making a long forward shot. He should be on the alert to create opportunities to develop an attacking play. When he goes up he should be careful not to get anchored up there but should come back at the first favourable opportunity—and come back fast.

TEAM PLAY

1.—The art of team play in polo is to create a situation that results in a score. This usually happens by a rapid reversal of the field by one player going down the centre of the field. Players should be on the alert to try to create such a situation. When they see that one of their own men is in possession of the ball or is going to gain possession of the ball, the other player or players should call to him for a pass. They should be continually striving to create such a situation. Other things being equal, a pass down the centre of the field is preferable to one down the side boards. The responsibility of creating such a situation falls on a man not in possession of the ball. As previously stated, a short wide pass is preferable to a long pass. The object of this play is to develop a long forward shot as quickly as possible. A back hand pass is easier to pick up than a pass under the pony's neck and should be used whenever possible.

2.—The players should interchange positions freely and should stay in the position they take until the play is completed. As soon as this is done they should be on the alert to regain their own positions as rapidly as possible.

BIBLIOGRAPHY

HORSEMANSHIP

A Guide to Basic Dressage, by Jean Froissard, London: Nelson.
Academic Equitation, by General Decarpentry, London: J. A. Allen & Co.
Basic Equitation, by Commandant Jean Licart, London: J. A. Allen & Co.
Basic Horsemanship: English & Western, A Complete Guide, by E. F. Prince and G. M. Collier, New York: Doubleday.
Breaking and Riding, by James Fillis, trans. by M. H. Hayes, London: J. A. Allen & Co.
The Complete Training of Horse and Rider, by Alois Podhajsky, London: Harrap.
Dressage: A Study of the Finer Points of Riding, by Henry Wynmalen, London: Pitman.
Effective Horsemanship, by G. N. Jackson, London: Compton Russell.
Equitation, by Henry Wynmalen, London: J. A. Allen & Co.
From Paddock to Saddle, by Capt. Elwyn Hartley Edwards, London: Nelson.
Give Your Horse a Chance, by Lt. Col. A. L. d'Endrody, London: J. A. Allen & Co.
Horsemanship, by Maj. Gen. Geoffrey Brooke (Lonsdale Library), London: Seeley, Service & Co.
Riding Logic, by W. Museler, London: Eyre Methuen.
Saddle Up, by Lt. Col. F. C. Hitchcock, London: Hurst & Blackett.
Schooling by the Natural Method, by Rolf Becher, London: J. A. Allen & Co.
Tackle Riding This Way, by Lt. Col. C. E. G. Hope, London: Stanley Paul.
The Manual of Horsemanship, by the British Horse Society: Kenilworth, British Horse Society.
The Riding Teacher, by Alois Podhajsky, London: Harrap.

STABLE MANAGEMENT

First Aid Hints for the Horse Owner, by Major W. E. Lyon, London: Collins.
Horse by Horse, A Guide to Equine Care, by D. R. Tuke, London: J. A. Allen & Co.
Know Your Horse: A Guide to Selection and Care, by Lt. Col. W. S. Codrington, London: J. A. Allen & Co.
Stable Management & Exercise, by M. H. Hayes, London: Hurst & Blackett.
T.V. Veterinary Horse Book: Recognition and Treatment, by The T.V. Vet, Ipswich: Farming Press.
The Horseman's Vade Mecum, by Michael Brander, London, A. & C. Black.
Veterinary Notes for Horse Owners, by Capt. M. H. Hayes, London: Hurst & Blackett.

THE GAME

American Polo, by Newell Bent. New York: The Macmillan Company.
    (This book provides a good history of the game in America. Chapter IX contains Hints for the Beginner, and an article by Devereux Milburn on the 'Science of Hitting in Polo'.)
As to Polo, by William Cameron Forbes. Manila Polo Club.
    (This book gives the 'Right of Way', or 'Column', game.)
Chakkar: Polo Around the World, text by H.R.H. Duke of Edinburgh, Lord Mountbatten, Rao Rajah Hanut Singgh, Juan Carolos Harriott, Jr., etc. Geneva.
Everybody's Polo, by Capt. James J. Pearce. London: Robert Hale Ltd.

BIBLIOGRAPHY

First-Class Polo, by Brigadier-General R. L. Ricketts. Aldershot: Gale & Polden, Ltd.
    (This book gives the 'Straight-to-Goal' game as played in Alwar, 1900-1903.)

Guide for Polo Umpires, by Capt. Wesley J. White. New York: United States Polo Association.

Hints on Polo, by Major F. Anderson, D.S.O., M.C. Allahabad: The Pioneer Press.
    (This book deals with team play and the care of polo ponies in India.)

Horse-Sense & Horsemanship of To-day, by Lt. Col. Geoffrey Brooke, London, Constable & Co.
    (Includes details on the conformation of polo-ponies and their training.)

Indoor et Paddock Polo, by Pierre Chambry, Paris.

Indoor Polo Association of the United States: Official Manual, New York: Polo Magazine, Inc.

In My Opinion, ed. by Major W. E. Lyon, London: Constable & Co.
    (Has chapters on Conformation of polo-ponies, training and hints for beginners.)

Modern Polo, by Lieut.-Colonel E. D. Miller, C.B.E., D.S.O. London: Hurst & Blackett, Ltd.
    (This book provides a good history of English polo up to the 'twenties and contains advice to beginners.)

Official Manual of the Indoor Polo Association of the United States, c/o U.S. Polo Association.

Polo, by the Earl of Kimberley. London: Seeley, Service & Co.

Polo in India, by Lieut.-General Sir Beauvoir de Lisle. Bombay: Thacker & Company, Limited.
    (This book gives the Durham Light Infantry Organisation, 1894-1898. It also contains useful advice on stable-management in India.)

Polo Ponies, by G. Cullum. London: Scribner.

Polo Pony Training with some Hints on the Game, by F. W. Ramsay. London: Gale & Polden.

Position and Team Play in Polo, by W. B. Devereux, Jr., with a foreword by Devereux Milburn. New York: Brooks Brothers, MCMXIV.
    (This book is based on the notes on which the Princeton Polo Team were coached.)

Practical Polo, by Lt. Gen. W. G. Vickers. London: J. A. Allen & Co.

Practical Polo, by P. O. V. Jubbulpore: C. H. Smiley, at the Mission Press.

The Lonsdale Library Book on Polo, London: Seeley, Service & Co. Ltd.
    (Includes chapter on 'Striking' by 'Marco'.)

The Training of Mount and Man for Polo, by the County Polo Association.
    (A small book to encourage beginners.)

Tournament Polo, by Beauvoir de Lisle. London: Eyre & Spottiswoode.

INDEX

NOTE: This Index only applies to the author's text up to and including Appendix II.

Advice, general, 84 *et seq.*
    to players individually, 81 *et seq.*
Aids, the, 6 *et seq.*
'All risks', 77, 87
Approach shots, 80
Attack, 75, 89

Backhanders, hitting, 42, 44, 48
    in defence, 77
    turning after hitting, 68
    turning to, 84
Ball, effect of a rolling, 50, 52
    out of play, 66
    topping the, 35, 36
Bandage, leg, 25
    tail, 25
'Barbs', 9
Bibliography, 183
Bit, the, 24
Blocking the goal, 85
Boots, for the player, 26
    for the pony, 25, 41
Brace, the, 33
Bran mash, 115
Bridle, the 24 *et seq.*
Burmese Tats, 17

Calling, by name for a pass, 107
    informative, 78, 105 *et seq.*
Cantering, 'disunited', 10
Captain, duties of the, 73 *et seq.*, 85 *et seq.*
    qualifications for a, 73
Centreing, 78 *et seq.*
Change of ends, 66
Changing legs, 10
    aids for, 11
China, ponies, 17

Chukka, the, 62
'Circular wind-up', the, 44
'Collecting', the pony, 8
Coloured band on sticks, 17
Combined practice, 81
Condition of pony, the, 113
Contact position, the, 38, 39, 44, 48, 51
Contented mind of pony, the, 116
Coverings for the handle, 18
Criticism by the captain, 73, 85
Crossing, 66 *et seq.*
Cupiss ball, 115
Curb-chain, fitting a, 24 *et seq.*
Cut, the, 31, 32, 53

Dangerous, riding, 68
    uses of the stick, 68 *et seq.*
Defence, 75, 76, 77
    scheme of, 88, 102 *et seq.*
Defenders hit over own back line, 70
de Lisle, General, 87
Diamond rule, the, 54
Direction, 80, 81
Discipline, off the ground, 73 *et seq.*
    on the ground, 73
'Disunited' cantering. *See* Cantering
Dress, 26 *et seq.*
Drive, the, 31, 32, 54
Duration of play, 62
Durham Light Infantry, 87

Exercise, 113 *et seq.*
Exercises, suppling, 4 *et seq.*

Feeding, 114 *et seq.*
First game, the, 70, 71
Flexibility in team play, 75, 76

INDEX

Follow through, 38, 44, 53, 55, 56, 57
Foot, under surface of the, 5
Forbes, Cameron, 87
Forearm, strengthening the, 6
Forty-yard hit, the, 70
   positions at the, 95, 105
Free hit, the, 70
   positions at the, 97, 105

Game, the 'column', 87
  the first. *See* First game
  mental picture of the, 61, 71, 84
  post-mortem after the, 73
  slowing up the, 89
  speeding up the, 89
  start or opening, 64
  the 'straight-to-goal', 87
Gloves, 41
Goal, blocking the. *See* Blocking the goal
   shooting at, 79 *et seq.*
'Green' pony, 3, 12
Grip, the, 33 *et seq.*
  the finger, 18
  the palm, 17
Grooming, 114
Grooms, 116
Guest Winston, 63

Handicapping, 63
Handle, types of, 17, 18
'Hands', 7
Head. *See* Stick-head
Health of the pony, the, 117
Hitchcock, Thomas Jnr., on Rules and Tactics, 180
Hit-in, the, 66
  positions at own, 97 *et seq.*
  position at opponents', 104 *et seq.*
Hitting, a 'safety', 70
  when mounted, 41 *et seq.*
Hooking sticks, 68, 69, 80
Horse, the wooden, 29

India-rubber rings, 23

Indoor polo, 63
Injury to pony, treatment for, 117
Interchange of positions, the, 75 *et seq.*

Lameness, care for, 14, 117
Layout of the ground, 61, 65
Leading leg, the, 10
Leading round a 'green' pony, 12
Loft and length in hitting, 49 *et seq.*
  positions of the ball for, 50

Mallet. *See* Stick
Manège, 6
Manila, 87
Martingale, standing, 25
Match play, horsemanship in, 13, 14
Meetings of the team, 74
Mental picture of the game. *See* Game
Momentum of the stick-head, 34
Mouth, the pony's, 7
  care of, 116
  improving, 8
  inside of, 5

Organisation, drawing up an, 87
  specimen, a, 89 *et seq.*

Pass, calling by name for a. *See* Calling
  waiting, and calling for a, 78
Passes, practising picking-up, 81
Pelham, 24, 116
Penalties, 70
  compared, H.P.A. and U.S.P.A., 177
Period, the. *See* Chukka
Pit, the polo, 27 *et seq.*
Placing the pony, 14
Plane of the swing, the, 34 *et seq.*, 39 *et seq.*, 53
Play, rough, 68
  starting to, 45 *et seq.*
Polo, the pony at, 118
  indoor. *See* Indoor polo
  pit. *See* Pit, the polo
  watching, to advantage, 61

INDEX

Pony, points of a, 5
  power, consideration of, 88, 108 *et seq.*
Position, the contact. *See* Contact position
  the rest, 32 *et seq.*
Positions, the interchange of. *See* Interchange of positions
Possession of the ball. *See* Ball
  man nearest enemy goal in, 101
Post-mortem after the game. *See* Game
Practice, combined. *See* Combined Practice
Pressing, 36
Pull, the, 31, 32, 53
Pulling pony, 8
Punctuality on the ground, 86

Referee, the, 62, 140
Reining back, 9
Rest position. *See* Position
Ricketts, General, 87
Riding off, 13, 71, 80
  school, 6
  without stirrups, 4
Right of way, 67
'Roughing-up', 118
Rules, History of the, 119
  H.P.A. Notes on the, 140 *et seq.*
  International, 119, 120
  International and U.S.P.A. compared, 177 *et seq.*
  the U.S.P.A., 152 *et seq.*

Saddle, 24
Schooling, 3
Seat, the correct, 4
S.E.V.A., 117
Shoeing, 118
Shooting at goal, 79 *et seq.*
Sixty-yard hit, the, 70
  positions at the, 95, 96, 105
Slings, the, 18 *et seq.*
Snaffle, the, 25
Specimen organisation. *See* Organisation
Speed, in attack, 89
  of the stick-head, 35

Spin, back, 51, 52
  top, 50, 51, 52
Spurs, 7, 26
Stable gear, 25 *et seq.*
Stable management, 113 *et seq.*
Standing martingale. *See* Martingale
Stick, care of, 23 *et seq.*
  choice of, 15, 16
  dangerous uses of. *See* Dangerous
  'feel' of, 15
  length of, 15, 16 *et seq.*
  materials for the head of, 21, 22
  materials for the shaft of, 21, 22
  recommended to the beginner, 23
Stick-head, momentum of, 35
  shape, dimensions and weight of, 19 *et seq.*
Stickholders, 86
Stick hooking. *See* Hooking sticks
Stirrup leathers, length of the, 4
Stirrups, riding without. *See* Riding
Stopping the pony, 8
Strengthening, the forearm. *See* Forearm
  the wrist. *See* Wrist
Stroke, the ideal, 34
  the near side backhand, 48 *et seq.*
  the near side forehand, 46 *et seq.*
  the near side under the neck, 55 *et seq.*
  the off side backhand, 42 *et seq.*
  the off side forehand, 37 *et seq.*
  the off side under the neck, 55
  timing the, 34, 40, 42, 45
Strokes, cut and pulled, 53 *et seq.*
  'fancy', 56 *et seq.*
  the four fundamental, 31 *et seq.*
  the twelve principal, 32, 53, 54
Strong, Sir Charles, 14
Substitution, H.P.A. directive on Rules re, 150
Suppling exercises. *See* Exercises
Swing, the, 34 *et seq.*
  learning the, 'by numbers', 36
  the near side backhand, 48 *et seq.*
  the near side forehand, 46 *et seq.*

INDEX

Swing *continued*
    the off side backhand, 42 *et seq.*
    the off side forehand, 37 *et seq.*
    the plane of the, 34
'Swinging' the pony, to turn him, 13

Tail bandage. *See* Bandage
Tats, Burmese. *See* Burmese Tats
Team, the, 61
    formation of a, 72
    meetings of the, 74
Team play, 72 *et seq.*
    the basic principles of, 74 *et seq.*
Thirty-yard hit, 70, 105
Throw-in, 64
    positions at own, 90 *et seq.*
    position at opponents', 102 *et seq.*

Timing the stroke. *See* Stroke
Topping the ball. *See* Ball
Turning the pony, 10

Umpires, the, 62
    H.P.A. Notes on, 140
    U.S.P.A. Guide for, 170
Under-surface of the foot. *See* Foot

Watering, 114
Whips, 27
Wintering ponies in England, 118
Wodehouse, Lord, xiii
Wooden Horse, the. *See* Horse
Wrist, strengthening the, 6